Parents Founding Charter Schools

Studies in the Postmodern Theory of Education

Joe L. Kincheloe and Shirley R. Steinberg
General Editors

Vol. 135

PETER LANG
New York • Washington, D.C./Baltimore • Boston • Bern
Frankfurt am Main • Berlin • Brussels • Vienna • Oxford

Patty Yancey

Parents Founding Charter Schools

Dilemmas of Empowerment and Decentralization

PETER LANG
New York • Washington, D.C./Baltimore • Boston • Bern
Frankfurt am Main • Berlin • Brussels • Vienna • Oxford

Library of Congress Cataloging-in-Publication Data

Yancey, Patty.
Parents founding charter schools: dilemmas
of empowerment and decentralization / Patty Yancey.
p. cm. — (Counterpoints; vol. 135)
Includes bibliographical references (p.) and index.
1. Charter schools—United States—Case studies. 2. Education—Parent
participation—United States—Case Studies. 3. Schools—Decentralization—United
States—Case studies. I. Title. II. Counterpoints (New York, N.Y.); vol. 135.
LB2806.36.Y25 371.01—dc21 99-055244
ISBN 0-8204-4908-3
ISSN 1058-1634

Die Deutsche Bibliothek-CIP-Einheitsaufnahme

Yancey, Patty:
Parents founding charter schools: dilemmas
of empowerment and decentralization / Patty Yancey.
–New York; Washington, D.C./Baltimore; Boston; Bern;
Frankfurt am Main; Berlin; Brussels; Vienna; Oxford: Lang.
(Counterpoints; Vol. 135)
ISBN 0-8204-4908-3

Cover concept by Patty Yancey
Cover design by Nona Reuter

The paper in this book meets the guidelines for permanence and durability
of the Committee on Production Guidelines for Book Longevity
of the Council of Library Resources.

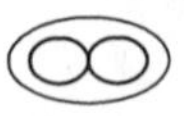

Printed in the United States of America

To my mother,
Frances Yancey

TABLE OF CONTENTS

TABLE OF CONTENTS

PREFACE

Few educational reform efforts in the United States have gained more momentum than the charter school movement, with 36 states plus the District of Columbia having approved legislation as of the year 2000. Interest was quite slow in building—only 100 charter schools were in operation three years after the first school opened in Minnesota in 1992. Moving into the millennium, over 250,000 students are enrolled in over 1,700 charter schools across the nation.

In theory, charter schools are deregulated, public schools of choice that can be created by a group of parents, teachers, community members, educators, and/or entrepreneurs upon approval by a state or local sponsor. Depending on the particular state law, the sponsor, and the local context in which the school operates, the degree of autonomy varies from charter school to charter school. Also contingent on state law, charter schools can be reconstituted from existing public or private schools, or they can be newly created.

This book explores the founding, development, and early operations of two parent-run, start-up charter schools. The two elementary schools, C-Star and Community Charter, are located in neighboring urban school districts in California.[1] They are identified as "parent-run charter schools" because the schools are founded or co-founded by parents and governed by boards of directors composed primarily of parents. Parents may or may not be employed by the organizations.

By limiting the study to one geographic location, the many local political factors that personalize and shape the founding process, development, and operations of charter schools become more visible. Ethnographic methods allow readers the opportunity to follow the evolution of external barriers that plague start-up charters in the early stages of the fledgling organizations and continue to affect everyday life for staff and parents after operations begin. The relationships between internal dilemmas—governance, staff turnover, and disenrollment, for example—and external barriers, such as state and district policies regarding start-up funding and the locating of charter school facilities, become clearer as the organizations develop over time. The method of investigation also allows a look at the various ways in which the backgrounds and motivations of parents can influence the founding process, educational vision, and organizational structure of the schools.

C-Star and Community Charter were struggling during the period of this investigation, and their founding stories are emotional roller-coaster rides of exhilaration and disappointment. The families and teachers involved began their charter organizing in the first years of the national charter movement when start-up funding and technical assistance were secured by mortgaging your house or recruiting the right parent. There were few examples to follow, and opposition from local school districts and teachers' unions appeared to be inevitable. The case studies of C-Star and Community Charter do not highlight glowing success stories. However, they do offer important lessons for families, teachers, and principals contemplating founding, enrolling, or working in parent-run charter schools.

NOTE

1. Names of schools, staff, and parents are pseudonyms.

ACKNOWLEDGMENTS

I would like to thank a host of friends and associates for their encouragement, support, and advice during this process. Among my colleagues at the University of California at Berkeley to whom I am particularly grateful for their input on my research are Pedro Noguera, Bruce Fuller, Eugene Bardach, and Paul Ammon. I would also like to express my sincere appreciation to Stacy Smith, Beryl Nelson, and David Ruenzel for their feedback, and to Susan Gilchrist for her technical assistance. Finally, I extend a heartfelt thank-you to the parents, teachers, and support staff of C-Star and Community Charter for allowing me into their schools and everyday lives in order to record their founding stories.

INTRODUCTION

> In the process—and I feel I can still say this after all the hours and work we've put in—I came to believe, and still believe, that even if the charter school never opens, it's been worth it to me. Individually, just having gotten involved with this group of people and reading the stuff I've read, it's just given me a much clearer idea about what I think is important about education and what I think is important about relating to kids. So even if this school never opens, it's been a big success that way. Wherever my son ends up going to school—this school, another public school, or even a private school—I'm going to have a much clearer idea about what matters to me.
>
> *Carl, Community Charter parent and founder*

Charter laws that allow parents, teachers, and community members to found and operate public schools challenge the hierarchical traditions of the public education institution. Although increased parent involvement in students' education has received much public press in the past decade, the character of that involvement is heavily bounded by professional educators' visions and desires of what parent participation in schools should be. Parents who have the power to make staffing decisions, evaluate administrator performance, and monitor financial expenditures have not traditionally been an integral part of that vision. Sarason, Brouillette, Fine, and Delgado-Gaitan, among others, have argued that a lack of trust in parents' abilities to make informed decisions, fear of multiple challenges to existing methods of practice, and threats to efficiency lie at the heart of this reluctance to share power.[1]

The two California charter schools that are the subjects of this ethnographic study are parent-run, start-up schools. C-Star and Community Charter were founded or co-founded by parents and are governed by boards of directors composed primarily of parents. The majority of the founders were motivated by their distrust of or disappointment in the public schools and believed that the state charter law held the key to an educational alternative. At C-Star, the founding parents were recruited by a professional educator who wanted to start her own school. They opened their doors in 1994 with 44 children enrolled in two classrooms, a kindergarten and a first grade. In contrast, Community Charter's parents initiated the founding process and petitioned for the charter on their own, without partnering with a professional educator. They opened their doors in 1997 with 65 children enrolled in two K/1 classrooms and one 2/3/4 classroom. Both charter schools planned to expand their enrollment and add grade levels in subsequent years.

The charter parents encountered many barriers in their quest to enter the formal decision-making arena of public schooling. Initially buoyed by the description of charter schools as deregulated public schools operating independently of their districts, the founders discovered that entrenched systemic standards and modes of operating schools—such as health and safety regulations, collective bargaining, accreditation, and standardized assessment practices—had to be addressed before petitions were approved or operations began. Depending on state, district, and other local determinants, some of these regulations and systems were negotiable, some were not. Other factors that posed significant problems were found in the individual, internalized norms among parents, teachers, and community members about what a real school is or what good educational practice means. The C-Star and Community Charter parents experienced, firsthand, that challenging the existing power structure of public education is one thing; "changing it is quite another matter."[2]

It appears inevitable that a disparate group of parents—inexperienced in the complexities of the education system or a public bureaucracy, in general—would encounter a fair amount of chaos and conflict in organizing and operating a school. Considering the complexity of the task and the time involved, why would parents even want to found and govern a charter school? Would they be able to participate with and be accepted as equals by teachers, administrators, school board members, and district personnel? As power shifts, or does not shift, among parents in the majority or in positions of authority within a charter school, how will the school's mission—the foundation of the charter petition's approval by the sponsor—remain intact? And, most importantly, can a group of parents with a mix of values, parenting styles and habits of mind work together to organize and operate a public school whose mission must encompass the interests and goals of the larger society?

The Charter Concept

The fundamental concepts underlying charters are that by freeing schools from the bureaucratic regulations that now inundate regular public schools—while holding educators accountable for student achievement and for the public funds they receive—schools will be created that are more efficiently run and more responsive to the families they serve. The more public school choices that are available will allow parents to exit their neighborhood school if they are dissatisfied and enroll their children in an alternative. Charter advocates argue that this introduction of market competition to public education will spur reform within an entrenched bureaucracy that has been so resistant to change. Reform will also be stimulated by the injection of "new blood" (i.e., parents, teachers, nonprofit and for-profit businesses) into the decision-making arena of an institution that has been monopolized by the rules and ideas of unions, school boards, and district superintendents.

The number of charter schools in a state, their range of educational programs and operational structures, and their potential impact on the surrounding schools vary considerably across the nation, reflecting the politics and the history of educational reform in each state, as well as the relationships between the state and its school districts. A state's charter law and the regulations that implement the law have a profound effect on the charter development process, how charters are granted, and how charter schools operate and relate to their sponsors. For example, in states that limit sponsorship of charters to local school boards and restrict the types of charter schools to pre-existing public school conversions, the possibilities for charter organizers are more limited than in states that allow a number of different public agencies to grant charters to start-up organizations as well as to preexisting public and private schools.

The state plays a primary role in determining what is possible in the charters under its legislation, but there are a host of local, social, and political factors that affect the founding process, development, and operations of the schools. The de jure situation mandated by law may differ from the de facto reality of how the laws are administered and implemented. This combination of state and local factors creates an *opportunity space* for charter organizers and operators that differs from state to state and from district to district.[3]

Not all state charter laws allow parents to be founders and chief operators of schools. For some charters, parent involvement is not a central issue due to the mission of the charter school or the population served (residential foster care programs, teenagers referred by juvenile courts, etc.). Nevertheless, the National Study of Charter Schools reports that nearly 50% of charter schools surveyed require some sort of parent or family involvement.

As the movement matures, researchers have noted that the ability of charter organizers to attract parents and students to these schools does not appear to be a problem. With the numbers of parents dissatisfied with their children's public schools, under-served students needing alternative public education solutions, and parents who are searching for school communities that reflect their personal values, charter enrollment continues to grow. But it is the actuality of significantly affecting student achievement and jump-starting change in traditional schools operating within the existing public school bureaucracy that remains a more complex and elusive mission for the charter movement.[4] The report card on student achievement in charters is still being tallied. Many states, including California, have not yet established solid assessment mechanisms to measure, monitor, and compare student achievement in charters vs. regular public schools.[5]

Total student enrollment in charters in 1997–1998 was less than 1% of all public school students across the nation. While some districts, such as Queen Creek in Arizona and Grand Rapids in Michigan, enroll high numbers of students in charter schools, many districts have few or no charters competing for students. And, as a 1998 Policy Analysis for California Education (PACE) study on the impact of charters on school districts explains, only districts that have a large number of charters appear to exhibit any response to their presence.[6] Districts that experienced low levels of impact generally exhibited minimal or no response. Factors such as the degree and climate of school choice within the district, overall student achievement levels, and district leadership appear to greatly affect the type of response to charters. The majority of district responses uncovered by the PACE investigation ranged from business-as-usual to the implementation of aggressive public relations campaigns. Only 24% responded "energetically" with actions such as offering more educational choices or reforming existing district schools (11, 20).

Outline

Chapter 1 provides an overview of the charter movement, with particular emphasis on California charter schools. I also felt it necessary to include a general discussion on parent involvement for those readers not well versed in this area of research. This section includes the influences of racial and socioeconomic factors on parent involvement patterns, as well as how school practices impact how parents relate to and interact with teachers and administrators.

In the second chapter, I detail the combination of organizational theories that provided me a means of understanding the peculiar phenomenon of a parent-run charter on multiple levels. Butler's thesis on organizational time, Levinson's work on role theory in the organizational setting, and Blau and Scott's classificatory scheme of organizations were pivotal in comprehending the interrelatedness of what was happening inside the charter organizations (i.e., roles, performances, and relationships of parents and staff) and the multitude of external forces influencing the functioning of the schools.[7]

Moving on to the case studies themselves, Chapter 3 graphically illustrates the painful struggle of C-Star parents and professional educators charting an alternative educational vision and "sharing" power. This first study also exposes the fragility of a charter school's founding vision when faced with changes in enrollment demographics and staff turnover after just one year of operation. In Chapter 4, Community Charter's long fight to receive charter approval was just the tip of the iceberg of external and internal barriers that founding parents encountered in their quest to form a school community that reflected their values. In both case study chapters, the impact of charter organizing and operations on individual lives and relationships, and the ways in which parent backgrounds and beliefs shape organizational life, are explored in-depth.

Generalizations across all parent-run charter schools cannot be made from these two case studies; nevertheless, in Chapter 5 some suggestions are posed that may be helpful for parents who are considering venturing into the process of founding and operating a charter school.

NOTES

1. Seymour Sarason, *Parental Involvement and the Political Principle: Why the Existing Governance Structure of Public Schools Should Be Abolished* (San Francisco: Jossey-Bass, 1995); Liane Brouillette, *A Geology of School Reform: The Successive Restructurings of a School District* (Albany: State University of New York, 1996); Michelle Fine, "[Ap]parent involvement: Reflections on Parents, Power, and Urban Public Schools," *Teachers College Record* 94.4 (1993): 682–710; Concha Delgado-Gaitan, "Involving Parents in the Schools: A Process of Empowerment," *American Journal of Education* 100.1 (1991): 20–46.

2. Sarason, *Parental Involvement*, 3.

3. RPP International and the University of Minnesota, *A Study of Charter Schools: Second-Year Report* (Washington, DC: U.S. Department of Education, Office of Educational Research and Improvement, 1998), 2.

4. Eric Rofes, *How Are School Districts Responding to Charter Laws and the Advent of Charter Schools?* Berkeley, CA: Policy Analysis for California Education, 1998. This study was conducted in 1997 and focused on 25 randomly selected school districts across eight states (Arizona, California, Colorado, Georgia, Massachusetts, Michigan, Minnesota, Wisconsin) and the District of Columbia. Data sources were interviews, written correspondence, and historical documents.

5. Amy Stuart Wells et al., *Beyond the Rhetoric of Charter School Reform: A Study of Ten California School Districts* (Los Angeles: UCLA, 1998).

6. Rofes, *School Districts.*

7. Richard Butler, "Time in Organizations: Its Experience, Explanations and Effects," *Organization Studies* 16.6 (1995): 925–50; Daniel J. Levinson, "Roles, Personality, and Social

Structure in the Organizational Setting," *Journal of Abnormal and Normal Social Psychology* 59 (1959): 170–80; Peter M. Blau and W. Richard Scott, *Formal Organizations: A Comparative Approach* (San Francisco: Chandler Publishing Company, 1962).

CHAPTER ONE

CHARTER SCHOOLS & PARENTS

> At points there is a redrawing of liberal concerns into conservative political policies. The call for choice is an illustration—a political and economic metaphor that maintains a broad symbolic appeal. The franchise model of education is related to the privatization occurring in other sectors of economy, culture and politics. Its main proponents argue that if parents choose the school that their children attend, market forces will produce motivation and achievement among those who previously had no choice.[1]

In 1988, Ray Budde's publication *Education by Charter: Restructuring School Districts* stimulated public interest in the concept of charter schools. The original model was a school-within-a-school that would be designed and operated by teachers who were granted the autonomy and flexibility to manage their own program.[2] The concept expanded from this model to include start-up schools, wholly reconstituted public schools and school districts, and reconstituted private schools. Under present laws, charter schools can be founded and operated by parents, teachers, community groups, businesses, or other organizations.

The charter school movement appeals to both liberal concerns and conservative pocketbooks, and seems to ignite a kind of "possessive individualism" across a diverse range of parents, teachers, and community groups. An ideology that promotes the individual citizen as proprietor of his/her own capabilities, "possessive individualism" is the theme that Thomas Popkewitz places at the heart of the "New" Federalism championed by Reagan and Bush.[3] Defining progress as "the sum of individual local political bodies" and characterized by a distrust of centralized authority, the New Federalism provides fertile ground for the school choice movement.[4]

It has been difficult for vouchers to gain the same bipartisan, broad-based support that charters enjoy because of the opposition's powerful argument that vouchers are a serious threat to the concept of free public education. While some charter advocates emphasize that charter schools will strengthen public education by expanding choice options, charter opponents argue that charter schools are just a forerunner of vouchers. In states such as California, where polls indicate that voters are seriously dissatisfied with the public schools and would support some form of vouchers, charter legislation appears to have provided a compromise.[5]

Although charter school proponents have linked their reform concept to the improvement of public education and have gained support across political, racial, and socioeconomic groups, critical questions that concern the purpose of schooling remain. In a 1994 paper about school choice, policy analyst Julia Koppich raised some key issues and posed important questions that charter advocates, practitioners, and sponsors must keep at the forefront of their thinking:

> A key public policy issue in the choice debate centers on the purpose of schooling. Parents and students have legitimate desires for educational choice. Society has a legitimate need for cohesion. Within a system of expanded choice, how is it possible to balance private benefits derived from schooling such as personal

> fulfillment and increased earning capacity, with the public interest associated with the education of preparing individuals to function effectively in a democratic society?
>
> If permitted to choose, is household preference for schooling aligned closely with racial, religious, or occupational status? Are socializing elements outside of school sufficient to meld together a society, or do we continue to rely on schooling as a major engine of social cohesion? Alternatively, has the nation grown so complex and diverse that we should abandon altogether the notion of a common culture and national social community?[6]

Some Characteristics of Charter Schools

The National Study reports that the majority of charter schools across the nation are small and newly created, with the median enrollment for all schools being approximately 132 students per school. In contrast, median enrollment for regular public schools in charter school states is about 486 students. The smallest charter schools are start-ups; the largest, converted preexisting public schools.[7]

In approximately seven out of ten start-ups, charter organizers reported that the reason for founding the schools was to "realize an alternative vision of schooling." Four of ten public school conversions reported that their reason for going charter was to gain independence from district and state regulations.

A prediction of opponents at the beginning of the movement was that charter schools would "cream" middle-class white families and middle-class families of color from the public schools, leaving low-income, poor children of color behind. Research indicates that charter schools operating in the 1997–98 school year did not disproportionately serve white and economically advantaged students. White students made up approximately 52% of charter school enrollment, compared to 58% of public school enrollment. Charter schools in Connecticut, Massachusetts, Michigan, Minnesota, North Carolina, and Texas enroll a much higher percentage of students of color than do all public schools in these states. Seven out of ten charter schools have a similar racial/ethnic composition to their surrounding districts, and 16% of charter schools enroll a higher percentage of students of color than their surrounding districts.

In California—the home of the two case study schools—262 charter schools enrolled approximately 100,000 students in the 1999–2000 school year.[8] State legislation allows charter schools to be either start-up organizations or existing public schools that convert to charter status. Charters are granted for a period of five years, after which schools must participate in a renewal process with their sponsors. Schools can lose their charters or not be renewed because of financial mismanagement, failure to meet student outcomes, or violations of the standards of their charters. As far as racial and ethnic composition is concerned, California charter schools are supposed to reflect the racial makeup of their surrounding school district. In the 1997–98 school year, the state's charter schools enrolled 48.1% white students compared to 39.5% in regular California public schools. African American student enrollment was 10.2% compared to 8.7% in other public schools; Hispanic student enrollment, 31.7% compared to 39.7%; Asian and Pacific Islander, 6.5% compared to 11.2%; American Indian, 1.8% compared to 0.9%. As far as low-income students are concerned, California charter schools enrolled 37% compared to 38% in other public schools across the state.[9]

Political Opposition, Negotiations, and Compromises

As mentioned previously, state charter laws are a result of the particular state context, politics, and viewpoints on how charter schools might be implemented. Which public agencies can grant a charter, when a charter must be reviewed and renewed by the sponsor, and whether charter schools can be start-up organizations or created from preexisting schools are the types of factors that are dependent on the state law. These factors greatly affect the charter *opportunity space*—what is possible for charter organizers. For example, if the local school board is the only authority that can grant a charter and if the school board, school district, and teachers' union opposition to charters is particularly high in that area, charter organizers may have a difficult time getting a charter approved. In California's original law, only local school boards were authorized to grant charters. If rejected, charter petitioners could appeal to their county board of education. The 1998 revisions to the law made it possible for charter petitioners to bypass their district and apply directly to their county board of education. If rejected, they could appeal to the state board of education.

In states where pro-charter legislators must bargain with powerful school districts and union opponents for passage of a charter law, "caps" limiting the number of charter schools (per state, per district, etc.) have sometimes been the compromise. California imposed a limit of 100 charter schools across the state—10 per district—in its original charter law. The cap was raised to 250 for the 1998–99 school year, with an additional 100 schools authorized for each following year. The district cap of 10 charter schools was also eliminated after the original law was revised in 1998.[10]

The California charter law was in its infancy at the time Community Charter and C-Star were petitioning their school boards. The original legislation specified that charter schools were not required to employ certified teachers; nor were they required to participate in collective bargaining, or have their teachers represented by the local teachers' union.[11] In the *First-Year Look at California's Charter Schools,* Southwest Regional Laboratories reported that all initial 34 schools in the state appeared to have strained relations with their local unions. "None of the charter schools that wanted to control hiring received the local teacher union's support (n = 8) for its charter petition while 61% of the schools (n = 23) where this control was not important received local union support."[12] Nineteen schools of the 34 surveyed agreed with the statement "A restrictive teachers' union contract is a major obstacle to charter schools" (36).

Relationships with local school districts and sponsors vary widely, ranging from district support in the development of charters to intense hostility from superintendents and school boards. Compared to start-up charters, preexisting public schools that converted to charter status reported far more difficulties with state or local board opposition, collective bargaining agreements, and state department of education resistance.[13]

Funding

The amount of public funding that an individual charter school receives and how funds are disbursed to the school are also dependent on the particular state law and the local district. The following summary of California's past and present funding system of charter schools barely scratches the surface of this complex issue, but it will provide an idea of how critical it is for charter founders and operators to understand the host of factors involved in calculating a school's revenue entitlements. The financial savvy, background experience, and professional connections of charter school founders and operators are key in increasing the amount of start-up and operating funds a particular school can access through negotiations with their district, through grant writing, and/or through personal loans.

Generally, the largest lump sum for California K-12 public schools—over 80%—is provided by the "Revenue Limit" system (also known as the Average Daily Attendance or ADA funding system), which is a combination of state aid and local property tax funds. Much of the remainder of funding for public schools is apportioned through federal categorical programs and local revenues.[14]

In the first years of operation, C-Star and Community Charter received their funding under the guidelines of California Senate Bill 1448. Under this law, California charter schools could choose from two finance models:

- Revenue-based. This approach was primarily utilized by start-up schools. The district serves as a conduit for the revenues generated by the students and programs at the charter school.

- Expenditure-based. Primarily used by public conversion charter schools, this approach "ignores funding entitlements and instead allocates resources to a

> charter school as if the school were a 'regular' district school."[15]

There were downsides and advantages to both models. For example, start-up schools choosing the revenue-based model did not receive the bulk of ADA funds until after February of the operating school year. Not receiving funds until after a school year was well underway had great implications for start-up charter schools. In states like California that offered no start-up funds for charters, organizers had to rely on grant-writing, personal credit, and donations to launch the founding process. Another serious drawback to the revenue-based model was that categoricals were not automatically available to the schools and had to be identified and bargained for by charter operators. As far as the expenditure model, charter schools operating within this funding system benefitted from economies of scale; however, the schools also contributed to the cost of district programs that were of no value to the charter school. In actual practice, charter organizers often negotiated with their districts for a combination of revenue-based and expenditure-based approaches.

Under Senate Bill 1448, the Superintendent of Public Instruction apportioned funds to each charter school as follows:

> (1) An amount for each unit of regular average daily attendance in the charter school that is equal to the current fiscal year base Revenue Limit for the school district to which the charter petition was submitted.
>
> (2) For each pupil enrolled in the charter school who is entitled to special education services, the state and federal funds for special education services for that pupil that would have been apportioned for that pupil to the school district to which the charter petition was submitted.
>
> (3) Funds for the programs described in clause (i) of subparagraph (B) of paragraph (1) of subdivision (a) of Section 54761, and Sections 63000 and 64000, [lengthy lists of state and federal categorical and special-purpose

> funding programs] to the extent that any pupil enrolled in the charter school is eligible to participate.[16]

The former funding law was complicated, but flexible, in that a large variety of financial arrangements were possible for charter schools.

In 1999, after many months of debate and deliberations, California revised the original legislation and established a new direct funding system for charter schools. The majority of the funds are from the Revenue Limit System and combine the state's general purpose and special purpose funding programs into a simple per student block grant. Charters have the option of receiving funds directly or through district accounts. The new law also attempts to simplify special education funding by presuming charter schools to be a branch of their sponsor district and directing special education funds to their district. As alternative options, charter schools can declare themselves independent of their districts or as an independent Special Education Local Plan Area (SELPA). These options, however, appear to be quite difficult to exercise without carefully negotiating with one's sponsor district.

In addition to the block grant, charter schools are eligible to apply separately for funds from state and federal categorical sources. Examples of additional state sources are Summer and After School programs, Economic Impact Aid, Elementary Grades Class Size Reduction, and the English Language Acquisition Program. Some of the federal application-based programs include Title I (based on the number of welfare-dependent families served) and Title IV (Safe/Drug-Free Schools). Because the application procedures for federal categoricals are lengthy and complicated, the California Department of Education advises charter schools that qualify for these monies to choose the option of receiving their overall funding through their sponsoring districts. This way, federal aid funds can be applied for in partnership with their districts.

For some schools, the 1999 system increases their funding, especially if the sponsor district retained a substantial percentage of funds under the old system. In other cases, however, charter schools will receive less under the new system. For example, charter schools currently operating in districts with high funding entitlements could lose because the block grant system caps funding at statewide average rates.

When the 1992 California charter law was enacted, the state made no provisions for charter school start-up monies. A loan system was eventually established, but regulations limited loans to a maximum of $50,000 and required that a school district apply on behalf of a charter school. The loans also had to be repaid within two years. A revision to that loan system was passed during the 1999–2000 California legislative session. Senate Bill 267 now allows newly created charter schools to apply directly to the California Department of Education for start-up loans, increases the loan cap to $250,000, and expands the repayment period to five years.[17]

Parent Involvement in Charter Schools

Not all charter schools place parents at the center of their mission, but those that do often require volunteer hours and service that are far more extensive than what is expected of parents in most public, private, and parochial schools. Nevertheless, the charter movement commands a large and fiercely loyal parent constituency. Parents and guardians report being integrally involved in the schools in areas that have traditionally been off-limits, such as student assessment, governance, and classroom instruction. Some participate in the founding of schools—formulating missions, goals and objectives, governance systems, and organizational structures. Considering the difficulties that teachers, administrators, and educational researchers cite as barriers to parent involvement in regular public schools—and even some parochial and private schools—why do charter schools garner such strong parental support and participation?

Some politicians and charter advocates argue that it is the element of choice that primarily attracts parents and guardians to the movement. However, educational researchers focusing on the broader issue of parent/community involvement contend that it is not simply choice, but a combination of institutional factors that contribute to high levels of parent involvement in schools.[18] These institutional factors include a greater sense of community, fewer regulations, and the ongoing development, assessment, and maintenance of programs that actively foster parent involvement. It does appear, however, that the power of choice situates parents in a much more central and powerful role with school administrators and teachers in determining the education of their children.[19] If there are alternatives available and parents can exit a public school with which they are dissatisfied, school personnel are more likely to pay attention to parental concerns, actively survey their level of satisfaction, and respond to their suggestions.[20]

Researchers from Southwest Regional Laboratories (SWRL) created a stir among charter school advocates in 1995 when they posed critical questions concerning the methods used by start-up schools (i.e., parent contracts) to encourage parent participation.[21] They suggested that "to some extent... [charter] schools are being organized to exclude students based on a new criterion of undesirability"—with "undesirability" defined as having parents or guardians who are not educationally involved and supportive (vii). Because the majority of charter schools receive no start-up or capital funding and no technical assistance from the government, parents are sometimes the major source of available labor for founding and maintaining the schools. Parents must also actively discourage absenteeism on their child's part to prevent a deduction in the ADA allowance for the charter school. Because of concerns regarding exclusion, California Bill AB 2737 was introduced to prohibit charter schools from requiring parent participation. The bill was vehemently opposed by charter school advocates and was eventually rejected by the California Assembly Education Committee.

Written contracts between the parents and the school at the time of the child's enrollment have become an accepted method of encouraging the level and type of parent involvement desired in charter schools. SWRL researchers suggested that parent contracts obtain compliance from parents and "permit schools more leverage over parents" (vii). The 23 parent contracts they analyzed listed parental requirements such as:

- Supporting and reinforcing school goals, philosophy, and practices

- Supervising and assisting with homework
- Supportive parenting practices (e.g., child nutrition, physical and emotional well-being)
- Participating in school-related activities (e.g., assisting in classrooms or working on committees)
- Discouraging student absenteeism and tardiness

Many contracts specified a certain number of hours that parents or guardians must volunteer for the school. These hours were spent participating at school functions or in the classroom, attending board or committee meetings, or assisting in school operations (office work, building maintenance, grant writing, etc.). Twenty-seven of the 34 charter schools (79%) in the SWRL report utilized parent contracts and 13 of 23 contracts reviewed contained "fail-to-comply" clauses. Penalties for noncompliance included fines and/or expulsion of the student; however, the most common identified consequence was "voluntary parent withdrawal" (17). SWRL noted that charter schools with "fewer parents in professional occupations and lower income, higher LEP, higher minority, and lower-achieving student populations are the schools more often using contracts with a fail-to-comply clause" (15).

Charter school advocates argue strongly that it is not only parental contracts and/or strict enforcement of requirements that garner high levels of parent involvement in the movement, but also the commitment of the schools to the families they serve.[22] Parents of C-Star and Community Charter echoed the leading reasons why parents choose a charter school as reported by the Hudson Institute in their 1997 study: smaller class sizes (53%), higher standards (45.9%), shared educational philosophy (44%), and more opportunities for parent involvement (43%).[23]

As far as more opportunities for parent involvement in charter schools, schools surveyed in the second year of the National Study (N = 383) indicated:

- 57.4% of charter schools (new and public/private conversions) offered parent education workshops.
- 64.8% of charter schools assigned staff to develop/monitor/foster parent involvement.

- 67.8% had carved out a powerful, central role for parents in the organizational structure.
- 65.3% maintained a log of parent participation patterns.
- 54.8% offered support services to facilitate parent attendance at meetings.
- 83% of the schools had parents involved in governance.
- 63.2% of the schools had parents involved in budget decisions.[24]

Charter schools are expanding the boundaries that have traditionally defined parent involvement in public schools. Although research over the last decade has documented the positive relationship between parent involvement and student achievement, public schools, teacher credentialing programs, and educational administration degree programs do not appear to have seriously revised their approaches to school governance or classroom policies regarding the involvement of parents.[25] In order to situate charter school philosophy and practices in the context of current research, a section on parent involvement in general follows.

Parent Involvement: An Overview

Significant improvement in student motivation, behavior, and cognitive development, as well as decreases in student absences and dropout rates, are some of the effects noted by researchers when parents take an active role in the education of their children.[26] Students whose parents actively participate in their education—helping with homework, attending school functions, serving on school committees, and so forth—exhibit higher academic achievement, regardless of socioeconomic factors. When parents exhibit support of their children's learning at home and at school, "'social capital' is created that produces normative support and legitimation for teachers' demands and more positive feelings on the part of children toward the school."[27]

The PTA was instrumental in identifying and establishing many parent involvement practices that are operating in schools and families today. The more traditional practices fall into two broad categories: parents' active awareness and interest in their child's personal well-being, and parents as supporters of the teacher's role and school functions. Two additional models of parent involvement that fall outside these two categories are "instrumental participation"[28] and "parent activism."[29]

Instrumental participation, defined as parent involvement in the decision making and governance of schools, situates parents in the policymaking role. Researchers have reported, however, that instrumental participation is "demographically skewed toward males, whites and high status groups"[30] and that parents "who need to be heard from most are disproportionately under-represented [on boards] following a standard election procedure."[31]

A more grassroots pattern of involvement is the parent activist model, which "is likely to be evident where there is urban socioeconomic and ethnic diversity."[32] Parent and community activism has in many ways driven the struggle for access and accountability for language minority and racial minority students. One of the earliest reported acts of parent activism was at the turn of the century when African Americans organized boycotts to protest having to attend segregated schools that offered only industrial training.[33] And, of course, the most significant parent challenge to the educational system, *Brown v. Board of Education*, led not only to the racial desegregation of schools, but also laid the groundwork for passage of the 1975 Education for Handicapped Children Act.

A contemporary standard of parental involvement is Wissbrun and Eckart's hierarchical model, which encompasses four levels of parent participation: spectator, support, engagement, and decision-making.[34] Parents' movement from one level to another varies in pattern—due to fluctuating or cyclical family and work demands—and is subject to frequent change. Dissatisfaction with a school's performance can sometimes cause parents who are operating at a low level of involvement to reassess their role and move up the ladder in order to become more influential in school policies and practices.

The first level of the model, that of spectator, is usually adopted by parents who themselves have had a negative or limited experience with formal schooling. Contact is minimal, and school-to-home communication is often unanswered, with some parents viewing the school as being primarily responsible for the education of the child. The second level, support, is the mode of involvement for the majority of parents and entails checking homework, reinforcing school behavior, monitoring attendance, responding to school communications, and so forth. In the third level, engagement, parents actively participate as volunteers in school functions and field trips and assume leadership positions to support schools. Principals and teachers are more active at this level in encouraging the relationship between family and school, and parents perceive a relationship of mutual trust and respect between themselves and the school.

At level four, decision making, parents operate as peers with administrators and teachers and are self-motivated to participate in the school community. In this situation, schools must share power with the parents and accountability increases. Educators and researchers caution that this power sharing can be carried to an extreme, causing a school's focus to shift to pleasing parents and "interfer(ing) with making decisions for the good of the child" (124). Wissbrun and Eckart warn that the decision-making process can deteriorate if this type of chaotic climate prevails. They posit that the ideal overall parent involvement scenario for a school would be all parents operating at the support level, a smaller number at the engagement level, and an even smaller number at the decision-making level.

Professional educators recognize the legitimate vested interest that parents have in their children; however, many do not believe that "that interest should be accompanied by the power to influence how schools and classrooms are structured and run."[35] Teachers and administrators often limit parent involvement to traditional support roles, which can be frustrating and demeaning for some parents and can affect the degree to which parents become involved with their child's school.[36] Toomey argues that typical parent involvement programs actually increase educational inequality because educators tend to favor those parents who willingly engage in participation patterns (auxiliary roles, teacher/parent conferences at the school site, etc.) sanctioned by the school.[37]

According to Rasinski and Fredericks, and Shepard and Rose, increased parent involvement can occur as a result of parents building trust in a school and the school community, learning more about the policies and practices, and acquiring the skills and knowledge necessary to increase their participation.[38] Dauber and Epstein report that the "strongest and most consistent predictors of parent involvement at school and at home are the specific school programs and teacher practices that encourage and guide parent involvement."[39] In their study of urban families in economically disadvantaged communities, parents reported little involvement in their child's schooling, at home or at school, if they perceived that the school was not interested in their participation. Regardless of the parents' education, family size, or the individual student's ability or grade level, parents were more involved if they believed that the school was trying to foster that involvement.

Socioeconomic, Racial, and Cultural Factors

In the last two decades researchers have been focusing more on the effects of socioeconomic, racial, and cultural factors on parent interactions with schools.[40] Findings reveal that parent involvement patterns of low-income, limited or non-English speaking, and inner-city African American families often mirror Wissbrun and Eckart's first level of the hierarchical model—the spectator level.[41] Parents may view the school doors as a barrier and not respond readily to personal communication with teachers and administrators.

A popular theory recently applied to the varying levels of parent involvement is Pierre Bourdieu's concept of *cultural capital*.[42] Annette Lareau applied the theory in studying low-income, white parents and their involvement with their children's schools. She found that the quality and quantity of parents' education, higher-income occupations, and social status provide them with a better understanding of school language, processes, and practices.[43] The families whose home lives mirrored the dominant culture's symbols, language, and authority patterns often shared the expectations and goals of the school institution. Schools affirm and reproduce the legitimacy of those practices associated with the dominant class culture by favoring those parents (and students) who reflect middle-class patterns of communication and "mainstream" policies of involvement. Middle- and upper-income parents whose social status is equal or higher in relation to the school staff operate in social networks that provide information on such things as innovative teaching practices and curricula, which affords them a higher level of confidence in intervening and influencing the quality of their child's education. These parents typically communicate often with school personnel and are comfortable volunteering at the school site.[44]

For many lower-income African American, Latino, and immigrant parents there is dissonance between their *cultural capital* and that of the dominant culture. This dissonance inhibits their sense of ease in operating within the school institution and too often results in an unquestioning acceptance of school practices. According to James Comer, these parents do not attend PTA meetings or participate in other traditional parent involvement activities because they feel uncomfortable at the school. His research in New Haven, Connecticut schools reveals that minority parents lack knowledge about school practices, harbor negative memories from their own educational experiences, and feel unwelcome when they do visit the school. Comer argues that schools must restructure involvement policies and mechanisms to attract those parents who feel mistrustful or uncomfortable with traditional school policies and settings.[45] However, as Toomey reports, alternative school involvement practices—such as home visits and off-campus parent meetings—that mediate this school/home *cultural capital* "clash" are often viewed unfavorably by educators because of the time and money needed to administer and implement such programs and the disbelief that the additional work will have any substantial effect.[46]

In cases of immigrant families with language difficulties and different cultural perspectives on educational roles, low parent involvement can also be the result of confusion as to the appropriate response.[47] Many Latino and Southeast Asian parents believe that maintaining a respectful distance from teachers and administrators is the proper and most helpful role they can play in their children's education. In some Southeast Asian cultures, individuals in public service are under obligation to the society at large to fulfill their assigned civic duties; therefore, educators are expected to assume full responsibility for the work that goes on in schools. The established educational role for parents is to supervise homework in the home.[48]

Other theories attribute low parent involvement patterns to the negative school experiences of parents when they were students themselves. John Ogbu argues that the racial stratification of African Americans in the United States has resulted in the development of a "deep distrust" for public schools, which affects "communication between blacks and the schools and black interpretations of and responses to school requirements."[49] The disproportionate number of low-income African American students who have been inappropriately referred to special education classes has done little to dispel parents' suspicions of institutionalized racism.[50]

For low-income parents, across racial and ethnic groups, the organization of their work lives and/or the daily stress of home life can dramatically influence the way the family functions, which can affect patterns of communication and involvement. Not having a flexible work schedule, a car, child care, or extra money for field trips can severely affect parents' time and patience in their interactions with school personnel.[51]

Rather than concluding that these parents do not care about education because of their limited patterns of involvement, researchers are asking if there are not more effective and systematic ways of facilitating parents' access to the social and academic resources they need that would allow them the opportunity to become better advocates for their children.[52] As Dauber and Epstein argue, "The schools' practices, not just family characteristics, make a difference in whether parents become involved in and feel informed about their children's education."[53] If this is so, why do urban teachers and administrators who actively solicit and encourage parental involvement report "that most parents are not involved and do not want to be"(69)?

Changes in the wider society—such as the frequency of both parents working outside the home and single-parent households—have also impacted the way families function, which affects patterns of parent involvement. Daily demands of family and the organization of work lives—for dual-income, middle-class families as well as lower-income families—yield little time or patience for school meetings, volunteering in the classroom, homework, or parenting workshops.[54] Claire Smrekar argues that this organization of work and daily life impacts parent involvement more than the amount of a paycheck:

> The layered responsibilities of parenting and employment turn typical evenings and weekends into tightly ordered time grids, with children's soccer practices, work meetings, and meals somehow squeezed into particular temporal slots. Cleaning up the kitchen after dinner, organizing bath times, returning phone calls, even reading the newspaper, seem to require immense amounts of effort and energy. (144)

Incessant daily demands also limit social contact with other parents at school, which can restrict networking between families. Due to the environmental factors associated with poverty (e.g., health and transportation problems, limited funds for extracurricular activities, and concern with personal safety) this insularity is compounded for low-income parents who are not employed. The general weariness and isolation that result from these factors severely affect low-income parents' opportunities of connecting with other parents to establish social networks and support that could help compensate for the environment's shortcomings. In addition to providing a channel to the latest educational programs and school news, this social support can "act as a buffer" and be "particularly beneficial for parents (and their children) in stressful circumstances."[55] Delgado-Gaitan and Ogbu posit that social networks established in the wider community, such as church and the workplace, can mediate the effects of insularity by offering additional opportunities for low-income Latino and African American families to consult informally with individuals who are more knowledgeable in school policies and practices.[56]

Effects of the Organization of Schools on Parent Involvement

Traditionally, many school administrators leave the work of "recruiting" parents to the individual classroom teachers. Parent-teacher conferences, soliciting classroom and field trip volunteers, phone calls and written notes about student behavior and upcoming programs are some of the most common methods utilized by teachers in establishing and maintaining relationships with parents. Parent involvement levels can fluctuate radically from classroom to classroom within a school because of teachers' differing communication methods, work styles, and assumptions about parents and students.[57] Moles argues that this fragmented approach can lead to communication breakdowns within the school institution and can contribute to parents' mistrust of a school's commitment to their child's success.[58]

Community has been a concept increasingly applied to school reform efforts to reflect participants' feelings of membership, trust, ownership, and psychological fulfillment.[59] Social scientists posit two concepts of community: functional and value.[60] Functional communities are characterized by a high degree of homogeneity—geographically, socially, economically, and ideologically. Value communities are more diverse as far as geographic, social, and economic factors, but members share similar ideals, attitudes, or goals. An example of a functional community used to be the Catholic school. However, due to societal pressures invading the once sheltered domain of this institution, the Catholic school is evolving slowly into a value community. Low- and middle-income parents seeking an alternative to public schools are choosing Catholic schools, not necessarily because they share the religion or live in the immediate neighborhood, but because of their *likemindedness*[61] as far as their educational goals and attitudes.[62]

Smrekar concluded from her case study of a more suburban Catholic school (317 students; middle- to upper-middle income; 75% white, 13% Asian, 8% Hispanic, 4% black) that the sense of community among the families enrolled was primarily the result of parents' exercising choice.[63] The paying of tuition was "the badge, the currency of commitment, that provided parents with a manifest sense of belonging to this community" (149).

Smrekar found a more "cohesive and robust" value community and better parent-teacher relations in a more racially diverse magnet elementary school that served 340 to 345 students from middle- to lower-middle-class families (49% white, 23% black, 14% Hispanic, 10.5% Asian, 3.5% Native American). She concluded that this was because of three institutional policies that contributed to a framework for a constructed community: required 40 hours per year parent participation; a three-way written contract among teachers, parents, and students; and an established network of communication channels. Rather than relying solely on "choice" to construct a value community, the magnet school employs "commitment" strategies, which create

> perfect redundancy: parents have an incentive to attend school events; the more events they attend the more relationships they form with other parents; and consequently subsequent occasions for face-to-face talk provide the opportunity to exchange information, thus providing additional incentives to attend school events. (146)

According to Simich-Dudgeon, schools that serve low-income populations with limited-English-proficiency (LEP) families should concentrate their parent involvement strategies on training families in tutoring activities and home learning reinforcement.[64] One parent involvement program that focused on training parents from four language groups—Spanish, Vietnamese, Khmer, and Lao—in tutoring strategies resulted in students achieving significant gains in English comprehension and paragraph-writing skills, fluency, vocabulary, grammar knowledge, and pronunciation. Over 350 LEP high school students and their families benefited from this project. One of the most important findings, Simich-Dudgeon reports, was that siblings and extended-family members often participated in homework activities. Parents explained that "although they wanted to help their children do well in school, they could not do so because they could not understand the language or concepts being taught to them" (198). This suggests that parent involvement strategies for various immigrant and low-income groups should be expanded to include cooperative learning at home with other family members. Parent and teacher surveys also indicated, as a result of the three-year project, that parents gained a better understanding of the school system and parental contact with schools increased.

Smrekar argues that there are three institutional characteristics of schools that can influence the experiences and expectations of families from different social classes. These can be interrelated within a school organization or can operate separately. When all three characteristics are operating interdependently at a school site, Smrekar reports that parent satisfaction and involvement are high.

- *Community.* Community is defined as a sense of solidarity or membership that benefits the individual as well as the group. The individual derives satisfaction and status from being a part of the group; the group benefits in terms of stability and social cohesion.
- *Choice.* Choice describes systems or policies that allow parents to choose the school their child attends.
- *Commitment.* Commitment refers to the programs and policies—teacher-initiated or school-wide strategies—that schools employ to develop and maintain parent involvement.[65]

As mentioned, "the strongest and most consistent predictors" of parent involvement patterns within a particular school community are the mechanisms that schools employ to encourage and guide parent participation.[66] Generalized assumptions about ethnicity and income level can be pitfalls that blind educators to inadequate or inefficient school policies that may be the cause of parent confusion, apathy, or alienation. Parent involvement programs that are not sensitive to the beliefs and values of different populations and exclude the voices of individual parents in the development of strategies often report little success.[67]

Neuman, Hagedorn, Celano, and Daly designed a study to elicit the opinions of young mothers about learning, while guiding them in their roles as educators of their children. Nineteen low-income, teenage, African American mothers whose children were enrolled in a free day care center were the subjects. The project instituted the practice of small, informal discussion groups for mothers and staff (10 hours total) at the day care center. Refreshments were served and the dialogue was free-flowing and nonthreatening. Although participants were racially and socioeconomically homogeneous, the researchers found considerable intragroup variability in beliefs about child rearing, learning, and literacy. The young mothers reported being isolated from other young parents and not having adequate opportunities to participate in conversations where information could be exchanged about parenting. Prior to the study, absenteeism was high at the day care center, and parent involvement was not an institutional commitment. The center provided few toys and books and no structured activities for the children besides meals and naptimes. The mothers attended weekly parenting education classes at their adult education program but did not transfer what was presented to interactions with their children.

As a result of the study, in addition to establishing literacy-related play centers (a kitchen and a grocery store) and a "cozy corner" library for the children, the day care center instituted ongoing training for mothers in their development as educators for their children. Regular, informal lunchtime conversations were instituted so that mothers could drop in and share information with staff members, researchers, and each other. The day care staff adopted a more open-door policy, inviting the young parents to spend time at the center playing and reading with their children. Many sessions were videotaped and used to coach the mothers individually in learning and literacy strategies. This practice proved far more effective in training parents than the weekly parenting classes at the adult education center. According to Neuman et al.:

> Through a better understanding of parental beliefs, parental involvement programs may be designed to enable culturally diverse parents to realize their aspirations for their children. But mutual respect is not enough; groups with diverse agendas need to identify shared goals and devise strategies for successful

> implementation. Parental beliefs may help shape certain school activities and policies; at the same time, these beliefs may inform school personnel of information and strategies that parents need for negotiating with schools. (822)

Preparation of Teachers and Administrators

Assumptions of school administrators and teachers about parent involvement and the strategies employed to encourage this involvement often do not take into consideration the multiple contexts within which families function, or their effects on families' daily lives. Traditionally unquestioned school practices, such as homework, can be just as burdensome and stressful for middle-class families with two working parents as for limited and non-English-speaking households. Whether the frustration lies in the limited time that families have to spend together after school and work or is the result of parents' educational limitations in offering assistance to their children, the practice can affect how parents feel and respond to their children's teachers and the overall functioning of the school.

According to Smrekar, "The rush to embrace parent involvement whole cloth without giving central consideration to the social context of family life has rapidly unraveled the authentic promise of parent involvement amidst persistent indications of negative and infrequent interactions between families and schools."[68] Preservice and inservice education of school administrators and teachers may include descriptions and statistics on the daily home and work lives of families, but very few programs explore how to modify, implement, and/or sustain parent involvement practices that consider the impact of these patterns on how families function.

Dealing with parents can be particularly challenging and demanding for administrators as well as for beginning and seasoned teachers. Teachers across surveys report frustrations with "uncooperative parents, uninterested parents, uninvolved parents, unhappy parents, noncompliant parents, untruthful parents, and lack of parental support."[69] However, interviews also revealed that preservice training of teachers included minimal or no information on how to work with parents or how to affect parent involvement.

One survey of teacher-training institutions in the Southwest found that only 4% offered a course on parent-teacher relations, and 15% provided part of a course.[70] However, when polled, 83% of teacher educators, 83% of principals, and 73% of teachers in the Southwest answered that a course should be required for undergraduate students in elementary education.[71] The major reason given for the lack of preservice courses is that the curricula for educational administrators and teachers are already so overloaded that "it is impossible to add additional requirements."[72] In a national survey polling parents' opinions on family/school interactions, 60% of all parents responding wanted schools to offer more guidance to teachers on how to involve parents more effectively.[73]

As mentioned previously, the question is not whether parent involvement influences student motivation and achievement, but how to develop and implement viable strategies to involve families across income levels, ethnic groups, and environmental settings. If these strategies do not reflect the social, cultural, and economic factors presently impacting families, they will most likely fail. Traditional institutionalized school practices such as homework must be critically reexamined, as well as the preservice and inservice education of teachers and administrators, in order to improve student outcomes for ethnically and socioeconomically diverse populations. In order for professional educators to develop meaningful, effective parent involvement policies, a "posture of reciprocity" must be established with the particular families they serve.[74] This would require

> a delicate shift in the balance of power between schools and communities. This power shift must be founded on a basic respect for families, their knowledge and beliefs, and their cultural community.[75]

Sarason adds, however, that this shift in the balance of power will more likely occur if parent and community involvement in schools has "legal sanction, the force of law."[76] In those charter schools where parents dominate governing boards, the balance of power has shifted, but not without discord and struggle. "When there is a change in power relationships one expects conflict."[77] Discord, conflict, and struggle are definitely at the forefront of the C-Star and Community Charter founding experiences. The "shift in the balance of power" in each case was far more difficult than parents and educators had envisioned.

NOTES

1. Thomas Popkewitz, *A Political Sociology of Educational Reform: Power/Knowledge in Teaching, Teacher Education, and Research* (New York: Teachers College Press, 1991), 141.

2. Marcella R. Dianda and Ronald G. Corwin, *Vision and Reality: A First-Year Look at California's Charter Schools* (Southwest Regional Laboratory, 1994).

3. Popkewitz, *A Political Sociology of Educational Reform,* 142.

4. Ibid., 152. In the 1980s decentralization and supply-and-demand philosophies began to gather steam in both the private and public sectors. Choice advocates carefully strategized to unhinge school choice from its racialized underpinnings and associate it with market principles. The concept also received a boost in support when the Reagan administration made the critical decision to soften its insistence that choice include private and parochial schools.

5. Julia E. Koppich, "How Californians View Public Education," *Educator* 8.1 (1994): 18–23. California voters defeated a statewide school voucher initiative in 1993 by a margin of 70% to 30%. Polls demonstrated that the defeat was due primarily to voters not liking the version of school vouchers available to them on that particular ballot. A 1993 poll conducted by the Policy Analysis for California Education (PACE) revealed that 63% of Californians supported the concept of school vouchers, 87% believed that the public schools must be changed, and 61% believed that the public education system was in need of a major, not minor, overhaul. Along ethnic lines, 72% of African Americans reported dissatisfaction with the public schools, compared to 58% of Hispanics, 63% of whites, and 51% of Asian Americans.

6. Julia E. Koppich, "Choice in Education: Not Whether, But What?" *Educator* 8.1 (1994): 6.

7. RPP International, *A Study of Charter Schools: Third-Year Report* (Washington, DC: U.S. Department of Education, Office of Educational Research and Improvement, 1999).

8. California Department of Education (Sacramento: Charter School Development Center, 1999), www.csus.edu/ier/charter/charter.html.

9. RPP, *Charter Schools*, 1999.

10. Amy Stuart Wells et al., *Beyond the Rhetoric*.

11. Under the 1998 California charter law, teachers who work in charter schools must be certified.

12. Dianda and Corwin, *Vision and Reality*, 23.

13. RPP, *Charter Schools*, 1999.

14. Eric Premack, *California Charter School Revenues, 1994–95: Laying the Foundation for Effectively Managed Independent Public Schools* (California State University, Sacramento: Center for Education Reform, 1994).

15. Ibid., 14.

16. Excerpts from Senate Bill 1448 (Chapter 781, Statutes of 1992) reprinted in Eric Premack's *California Charter School Revenues, 1994–95.*

17. Much of this information on California's funding revisions for charter schools was radically condensed from Eric Premack's *1999 Preliminary Overview: New Charter School Funding System, Special Education, and Attendance Accounting Laws* (Sacramento: Charter School Development Center, 1999), www.csus. edu/ier/charter/charter.html. I suggest readers access this website for a more detailed explanation of California's approach to funding charter schools.

18. Claire Smrekar, *Impact of School Choice and Community* (Albany: State University of New York Press, 1996); Concha Delgado-Gaitan, "Involving Parents in the Schools: A Process of Empowerment," *American Journal of Education* 100.1 (1991): 20–46.

19. Joe Nathan, *Charter Schools: Creating Hope and Opportunity for American Education* (San Francisco: Jossey-Bass Publishers, 1996); Bruce Fuller and Richard Elmore, *Who Chooses, Who Loses? Culture, Institutions, and the Unequal Effects of School Choice* (New York: Teachers College Press, 1996); Paul Peterson, "The New Politics of Choice," in *Learning from the Past: What History Teaches Us about School Reform*, eds. Diane Ravitch and Maris A. Vinowskis (Baltimore: The Johns Hopkins University Press, 1995), 217–42.

20. Nathan, *Charter Schools.*

21. Henry J. Becker, Kathryn Nakagawa, and Ronald G. Corwin, *Parent Involvement Contracts in California's Charter Schools: Strategy for Educational Improvement or Method of Exclusion?* (Los Alamitos, CA: Southwest Regional Laboratory, 1995). C-Star was going into its first year of operations and the Community Charter founders were petitioning their school board for approval at the time the SWRL report was released.

22. Nathan, *Charter Schools.*

23. Gregg Vanourek et al., *Charter Schools in Action. Final Report, Part 1* (Washington, DC: Hudson Institute, 1997).

24. Phone survey data from the National Study of Charter Schools, 1998.

25. Seymour Sarason, *Revisiting "The Culture of the School and the Problem of Change"* (New York: Teachers College Press, 1996).

26. Susan L. Dauber and Joyce L. Epstein, "Parents' Attitudes and Practices of Involvement in Inner-City Elementary and Middle Schools," in *Families and Schools in a Pluralistic Society*, ed. Nancy F. Chavkin (Albany: State University of New York Press, 1993), 53–71; Anne Henderson, *The Evidence Continues to Grow: Parent Involvement Improves Student Achievement* (Columbia, MD: National Committee for Citizens in Education, 1987); John Ogbu, "Origins of Human Competence: A Cultural-Ecological Perspective," *Child Development* 52 (1981): 413–29; James P. Comer, *School Power* (New York: New York University Press, 1980); Urie Bronfenbrenner, *Is Early Intervention Effective: A Report on Longitudinal Evaluations of Preschool Programs*, vol. 2 (Washington, DC: Department of Health, Education, and Welfare, 1974).

27. James Coleman, "Families and Schools," *Educational Researcher* 16 (1987): 32–38, cited by Becker, Nakagawa, and Corwin, *Parent Involvement*, 1.

28. Robert Holt Salisbury, *Citizen Participation in the Public Schools* (Lexington, MA: Lexington Books, 1980).

29. W. Perry and M. D. Tannenbaum, "Parents, Power, and the Public Schools," in *Education and the Family*, ed. Leonard Kaplan (Needham Heights, NJ: Allyn and Bacon, 1992), 100–15.

30. Ibid., 108.

31. D. E. Kapel and W. T. Pink, "The Schoolboard: Participatory Democracy Revisited," *Urban Review* 10 (1978): 21.

32. Perry and Tannenbaum, "Parents," 108.

33. Ibid.

34. D. Wissbrun and J. A. Eckart, "Hierarchy of Parental Involvement in Schools," in *Education and the Family*, ed.

Leonard Kaplan (Needham Heights, NJ: Allyn and Bacon, 1992), 119–31.

35. Sarason, *Parental Involvement*, 20.

36. Henderson, *Evidence.*

37. D. Toomey, "Home-School Relations and Inequality in Education," address to Conference on Education and the Family, Brigham Young University, 1986.

38. T. V. Rasinski and A. D. Fredericks, "Working with Parents: Dimensions of Parent Involvement," *The Reading Teacher* 43 (1989): 180–82; Richard Shepard and Harold Rose, "The Power of Parents: An Empowerment Model for Increasing Parental Involvement," *Education* 115 (1995): 373–77.

39. Dauber and Epstein, "Parents' Attitudes and Practices," 61.

40. Concha Delgado-Gaitan, "School Matters in the Mexican-American Home: Socializing Children to Education," *American Educational Research Journal* 29.3 (1992): 495–513; P. LeBlanc, "Parent-School Interactions," in *Education and the Family*, ed. Leonard Kaplan (Needham Heights, NJ: Allyn and Bacon, 1992), 132–40; J. Maddaus, "Worlds Apart or Links Between: Theoretical Perspectives on Parent-Teacher Relationships" (paper presented at the annual meeting of the American Educational Research Association, Chicago, IL, 1991); Annette Lareau, *Home Advantage: Social Class and Parental Intervention in Elementary Education* (New York: Falmer, 1989); James P. Comer, "Educating Poor Minority Children," *Scientific American* 259 (1988): 42–48; M. S. Kohn, "Social Class and Parent-Child Relationships," in *Sociology of the Family*, ed. M. Anderson (Middlesex, UK: Penguin Books, 1971).

41. Wissbrun and Eckart, "Hierarchy of Parental Involvement"; Delgado-Gaitan, "School Matters"; X. C. Tran, *The Factors Hindering Indochinese Parent Participation in School Activities*

(San Diego, CA: San Diego State University, Bilingual Education Service Center, Institute for Cultural Pluralism, 1982); Ogbu, "Origins of Human Competence."

42. Lareau, *Home Advantage;* Smrekar, *Impact of School Choice.* Pierre Bourdieu defines the concept of *cultural capital* as the overall cultural background, makeup, ways of living, knowledge, and skills that are passed on from generation to generation. In his theory, children of the upper classes inherit a very different cultural capital than working-class children. Children who grow up in families that frequent museums, read books, have libraries in the home, attend live theater, and engage in other such practices acquire a familiarity with the dominant culture that is valued by schools. Children whose families are on the margins and do not engage in such practices, or engage in them infrequently, are at a disadvantage. See Bourdieu, "Cultural Reproduction and Social Reproduction," in *Power and Ideology in Education,* ed. J. Karabel and A. H. Halsey (New York: Oxford University Press, 1977).

43. Lareau, *Home Advantage.*

44. Ibid.; Delgado-Gaitan, "School Matters."

45. Comer, "Educating Poor Minority Children."

46. Toomey, "Home-School Relations."

47. Delgado-Gaitan, "School Matters."

48. Tran, *Factors Hindering Indochinese Parent Participation.*

49. John Ogbu, "Racial Stratification and Education in the United States: Why Inequality Persists," *Teachers College Record* 96.2 (1994): 264–98, 291.

50. Office of Civil Rights, *1980 Elementary and Secondary School Survey* (Washington, DC: Office of Civil Rights, US Department of Education, 1982).

51. Smrekar, *Impact of School Choice.*

52. Ibid.; Delgado-Gaitan, "School Matters"; B. L. Sung, *Chinese Immigrant Children in New York City* (New York: Center for Migration Studies, 1987).

53. Dauber and Epstein, "Parents' Attitudes," 61.

54. Smrekar, *Impact of School Choice;* W. R. Houston and E. Houston, "Needed: A New Knowledge Base in Teacher Education," in *Education and the Family,* ed. Leonard Kaplan (Needham Heights, NJ: Allyn and Bacon, 1992), 255–65.

55. Victor Battistich, Daniel Solomon, Dong-il Kim, Marilyn Watson, and Eric Schaps, "Schools as Communities, Poverty Levels of Student Populations, and Students' Attitudes, Motives, and Performance: A Multilevel Analysis," *American Educational Research Journal* 32.3 (1995): 627–58, 650.

56. Delgado-Gaitan, "School Matters"; John Ogbu, "Understanding Cultural Diversity and Learning," *Educational Researcher* 21.8 (1992): 5–14.

57. Joyce L. Epstein and Susan L. Dauber, "Teacher Attitudes and Practices of Parent Involvement in Inner-City Elementary and Middle Schools" (paper presented at the annual meeting of the American Sociological Association, Atlanta, GA, 1988).

58. Oliver C. Moles, "Collaboration Between Schools and Disadvantaged Parents: Obstacles and Openings," in *Families and Schools in a Pluralistic Society,* ed. Nancy F. Chavkin (Albany: State University of New York Press, 1993), 21–49.

59. Battistich et al., "Schools as Communities"; Martin Haberman, "Creating Community Contexts That Educate: An Agenda for Improving Education in Inner Cities," in *Education and the Family,* ed. Leonard Kaplan (Needham Heights, NJ: Allyn and Bacon, 1992), 27–40; David W. MacMillan and David M. Chavis, "Sense of Community: A Definition and Theory," *Journal of Community Psychology* 14 (1986): 6–23.

60. Haberman, "Creating Community Contexts"; Smrekar, *Impact of School Choice;* James E. Coleman and Thomas Hoffer, *Public and Private High Schools: The Impact of Communities* (New York: Basic Books, 1987).

61. John Dewey, *Democracy and Education 1916* (Carbondale: Southern Illinois University Press, 1985). Dewey believed that the nucleus of a community [*likemindedness*] is formed by shared "aims, beliefs, aspirations, knowledge—a common understanding. ... Such things cannot be passed physically from one to another, like bricks; they cannot be shared as persons would share a pie by dividing it into physical pieces. The communication which insures participation in a common understanding is one which secures similar emotional and intellectual dispositions—like ways of responding to expectations and requirements," 7.

62. Bruce Fuller, "Which School Reforms are Politically Sustainable and Locally Effective? The Contextual Influence of Cultural Pluralism" (paper presented at the University of California, Berkeley, Graduate School of Education, April, 1995). In Milwaukee and San Antonio, where two school-choice experiments are presently operating, low-income parents can apply for vouchers (equaling the per student spending level observed in the states) that can be used to enroll their children at any private or parochial school. San Antonio's program was initiated in 1983 and Milwaukee's in 1990. Both citywide programs were established as a response to the low-income ethnic communities' dissatisfaction with student outcomes in the regular public school system. The majority of the participants in the programs are

working-class and poor families earning less than $25,000 per year. In Milwaukee, many of the participating families are headed by single mothers who are on, or recently off, welfare. Researchers of these two voucher programs are finding that parents who were already actively invested in their children's education—prior to the voucher initiatives—comprise the majority of the families participating. The students left behind in the neighborhood public schools are the children of parents who are absent or minimally involved.

63. Smrekar, *Impact of School Choice.*

64. Carmen Simich-Dudgeon, "Increasing Student Achievement through Teacher Knowledge about Parent Involvement," in *Families and Schools in a Pluralistic Society,* ed. Nancy F. Chavkin (Albany: State University of New York Press, 1993), 189–203.

65. Smrekar, *Impact of School Choice.*

66. Dauber and Epstein, "Parents' Attitudes," 61.

67. Susan B. Neuman, Tracy Hagedorn, Donna Celano, and Pauline Daly, "Toward a Collaborative Approach to Parent Involvement in Early Education: A Study of Teenage Mothers in an African-American Community," *American Educational Research Journal* 32.4 (1995): 801–27; Michelle Fine, "[Ap]parent Involvement: Reflections on Parents, Power, and Urban Public Schools," *Teachers College Record* 94.4 (1993): 682–710.

68. Smrekar, *Impact of School Choice,* 2.

69. W. R. Houston and J. L. Williamson, *Perceptions of Their Preparation by 42 Texas Elementary School Teachers Compared with Their Responses as Student Teachers* (Houston, TX: University of Houston, 1990), 257.

70. Moles, "Collaboration."

71. Ibid.

72. F. Kochan and B. K. Mullins, "Teacher Education: Linking Universities, Schools, and Families for the 21st Century," in *Education and the Family,* ed. Leonard Kaplan (Needham Heights, NJ: Allyn and Bacon, 1992), 266–72, 272.

73. Moles, "Collaboration."

74. Harry, 1992, quoted by Neuman et al., "Collaborative Approach."

75. Neuman et al., "Collaborative Approach," 822.

76. Sarason, *"Revisiting,"* 335.

77. Sarason, *Parental Involvement,* 13.

CHAPTER TWO

METHODOLOGY

Ethnographic methods were used to investigate the founding and early operations of two parent-run, start-up charter schools. The two elementary schools are located in neighboring districts and were among the first wave of charters approved under the 1992 California charter law.

Qualitative data—interviews, observations, and documents—were collected over a period of approximately two years at C-Star (November 1994 through October 1996); and two and a half years at Community Charter (October 1995 through February 1998). The majority of interviews and meeting observations were audio recorded and transcribed; field notes were always taken as a backup measure. When acoustics were marginal or when respondents were not agreeable to being recorded, only field notes were taken.

The primary respondents and foci of the investigation are the parents of children who were enrolled or planned to be enrolled in the two charter schools. Additional participants included the professional educators who were employed by the two charter schools (teachers, coordinators, consultants, and directors/principals); school district personnel and board members; county education personnel and board members; and teachers' union personnel.

C-Star

When I started my investigation of C-Star, the charter school was in its third month of operations. There were 44 children enrolled in two classrooms, a kindergarten and a first grade. I was allowed access as a researcher in exchange for volunteering in the classrooms one day per week. For seven months I volunteered and attended staff, board, and parent meetings. I also interviewed staff members, parents, and district personnel. Follow-up interviews with some of the staff and parents were conducted during the summer months. A journal of field briefs, questions, working hypotheses, and general notes was kept during the period of data collection. For the first year, field briefs were written after each observation.

Many of the problems observed in the relationships between parents, between staff, and between parents and staff that first year appeared to be rooted in the planning stages of the organization. Because I was not on site until the third month of operations, I researched the planning stage and first two months of operations through historical documents (i.e., meeting notes, newspaper articles, memos, and letters) and interviews. I presented a paper at the 1997 AERA annual meeting detailing the internal conflict that occurred between the educational leader and the parents in the first year of operations.[1] Key findings of that paper were:

- Because their desire to escape the traditional public school system was so strong and their choices were so few, parents were willing to ignore serious doubts they experienced early on about the educator who was leading the charter school founding process.

- The second lead motivator in joining together to form C-Star was the desire of parents to be a part of a community that was involved in collective work.

- Many parents exhibited signs of *social loafing* in their passive acceptance of the content of the charter petition and governance issues until they became aware of problems in the classroom, and conflicts escalated between staff and more involved parents.[2]

- After the school doors opened and classroom practices appeared radically different from the internalized norm of "real school" (i.e., teacher-centered pedagogy and homework), parents began to question the validity of the educational program and the professional qualifications of the educational leader/ head teacher.

- As the interpersonal strife escalated after operations began, external concerns such as fund-raising and district accountability demands were set aside, seriously impacting the viability of the organization. There were no systems in place to deal with grievances and those that were proposed, after conflict surfaced, were viewed with skepticism and mistrust by opposing factions.

These findings influenced my decision to continue research at C-Star for another year and to conduct another investigation of a parent-founded charter school, firsthand, during the period before petition approval through the initial stages of operations. I gained access to Community Charter, a parent start-up in a neighboring city that was in the petitioning phase of its development, while continuing my study of C-Star.

In the second year at C-Star, I conducted interviews with district personnel, school board members, an educational consultant contracted by C-Star, and families who had chosen not to return to C-Star. Observations on site were limited to a series of meetings between February and May 1996. Interviews with parents were conducted primarily over the phone and continued through the fall of 1996. Journal entries were recorded after interviews and observations.

All interview audio tapes were transcribed. Select portions of meetings were transcribed after listening to audio tapes and after critical incidents were coded in field notes. Data collection details appear in Appendix A.

Community Charter

I mailed a letter of introduction to Community Charter in September of 1995. At the time, the parents were preparing for their third petition hearing. Having been rejected twice by its district sponsor, Community Charter was preparing to petition the county for charter status at the time I began observing their developmental process. The founding group was composed solely of parents, with the original seven parents still integrally involved in the petitioning process.

In exchange for permission to conduct the study, I agreed to assist the group by supplying current information on general developments in the national and state charter movement and in educational programming, as needed. Because of the professional backgrounds (i.e., lawyers, development directors, teachers) and the wide range of higher education degrees among the Community Charter membership, I possessed little information that was not readily available to someone in the group. On several occasions I agreed to serve as timekeeper or as an impartial facilitator for meetings where heated topics were under discussion.

For the first eight months, the primary method of data collection was through participant and nonparticipant observation of meetings (for example, general charter, interim board, special work, and committee meetings; county meetings and public hearings). Interviews with founders and particularly active members, as well as with district and union personnel, were conducted by phone and in person. Phone interviews continued through the summer months. Field briefs were written after each observation and journal entries were made weekly during this period.

The following school year—the interim year before charter school operations began—I attended three meetings, made visits to the site and immediate neighborhood, conducted phone interviews with parents who had left the group and with district, county, and union personnel. Data collection this year focused on documents and phone interviews. The bulk of interviews were with parents who had left the group. Immediately prior to the charter school opening, I made another site visit and brief, separate interviews were conducted with staff on site. I wrote field briefs after observing the meetings and in-school activities during this period of data collection.

In the third year, Community Charter opened with 65 children enrolled in two K/1 classrooms and one 2/3/4 classroom. I spent one day on site, the week before school opened, to observe preparations and to talk with staff. After school opened, I observed classrooms and school operations for two days, and attended back-to-school night and a fund-raiser off-site. The primary source of data was through interviews (via phone and face-to-face) with new and returning parents and with county personnel. One county board member was interviewed. Field briefs were written after each observation and weekly journal entries were made during this period of data collection. Data collection specifics appear in Appendix B.

Study Design

A combination of methodological and theoretical approaches were used as guides for data collection and analysis in order to investigate the phenomenon of the charter school as a business organization, a community, a public school, and a new educational reform effort. Erickson's "interpretive" approach to qualitative methods in teacher research and Blau and Scott's thesis on the study of formal organizations were utilized to design the approach to data collection.[3] For data analysis a hybrid of four methods was used:

- First, Miles and Huberman's "time ordered display" was used to construct a visual picture or diagram of the data.[4]
- Butler's theory of time in the study of decision-making and learning in organizations provided a

means of analyzing how the charter work (which changed character along the developmental time line) defined the organizational experience for parents.[5]
- Levinson's organizational role theory shaped the investigation of individual parents' roles within the charter organization, their influence on the development of the organization, and the impact of the process on individual members.[6]
- Finally, Blau and Scott's *cui bono* typology of organizations provided a strategy for overlaying broader issues, such as school choice and decentralization into the analysis.[7]

Data Collection

"Interpretive," in Erickson's definition, refers to "the whole family of approaches to participant observational research" (e.g., ethnographic, case study, phenomenological).[8] The research lens is focused on "the relation between meaning perspectives of actors and the ecological circumstances of action in which they find themselves" (127). Although Erickson's emphasis is on the teacher in the classroom, he posits interpretive methods as most appropriate when one is trying to discover ways in which local and nonlocal forms of social organization and culture relate to the activities of specific persons in making choices and conducting social action together. According to him, participant observational fieldwork is "best at answering the following questions":

- What is happening, specifically, in social action that takes place in this particular setting?
- What do these actions mean to the actors involved in them, at the moment the actions took place?
- How are the happenings organized in patterns of social organization and learned cultural principles for the conduct of everyday life—how, in other words, are people in the immediate setting consis-

tently present to each other as environments for one another's meaningful actions?

- How is what is happening in this setting as a whole related to happenings at other system levels outside and inside the setting?
- How do the ways everyday life in this setting is organized compare with other ways of organizing social life in a wide range of settings in other places and at other times? (121)

In the first year of data collection with each charter school group, my interaction with members was frequent. For example, in addition to conducting interviews at C-Star, I volunteered one full day a week and attended all staff meetings and parent meetings. This frequency of contact and familiarity with the C-Star community allowed me to experience the action more as an "actor" or participant observer. Because Community Charter was in the preoperational stage when I gained entry, volunteering for the school was not an option. However, there were numerous meetings where the majority of members were strategizing and interacting, which allowed me the opportunity to experience the ecology of the parent group. After the first year with each charter, I assumed the role of a nonparticipant observer and restricted my involvement to observing at general meetings, strategic board and committee meetings, school events, and in classrooms.

In Blau and Scott's approach to data collection techniques in the study of organizations, they promote field study as the method "for providing an overall picture of the organization and information about the interdependence of its constituent parts."[9] Nonparticipant observation, face-to-face interviews (unstructured and structured), and the analysis of documents facilitate the examination of nuances between personal beliefs and public behavior of the participants in organizations. Blau and Scott emphasize the "particular advantage" of the "natural resources" available to the researcher in the study of formal organizations: records, manuals of operation, reports, and so forth (18). In the C-Star and Community Charter case studies, the analysis of documents (e.g., the charter petitions, bylaws, public flyers and announcements, correspondence to/from sponsors and union officials, local news articles) and interviews was imperative in the linkage of behaviors and actions observed firsthand to decisions and incidents that occurred prior to my gaining entry to the site. Because of the difficulty encountered in scheduling a broader range of interviews with public officials and district staff members, document analysis was important in developing an understanding of the dynamics between the charter schools and their sponsors and their surrounding communities.

For the first year of data collection with each of the two charter school groups, six to ten hours per week were spent observing (participant and nonparticipant observation) school-related meetings, volunteering in the classrooms, and/or conducting interviews. This contact was motivated by the desire to establish trust and familiarity with the parents and staff so that informal interactions could be observed with as little focus on the researcher as possible. Interviews were conducted with parents and staff, as well as public school officials and district and county personnel. After the initial year of observation of each charter school group, contact with parents was characterized primarily by individual face-to-face interviews, phone interviews, e-mail correspondence, and small, informal focus groups. School meetings and activities were still attended, but not as regularly as in Year One.

Data Analysis

A time line was constructed for each case study, with information grouped and coded according to the developmental stage of occurrence—initial recruitment/establishing the mission; petitioning the sponsor; after approval/preoperations; early operations. C-Star's time line included the second year of operations. Within the organizational stages of the charter schools were "critical incidents" that were particularly important to each (i.e., negotiations with sponsor, defining the organizational and governance structures, location of site, hiring and evaluating of personnel).[10] How decisions were made, how tasks were accomplished, and the roles of individual parents (or groups of parents) in decision making and the accomplishment of tasks related to these critical incidents were noted. Links were made between specific incidents, the major players, and the conditions or "states" that developed or were experienced by the group.[11] Links were also made between developmental stages to assess lingering effects of prior critical incidents on the functioning of the overall organization.

In charting and analyzing the developmental stages of the charter schools, the issue of "time" repeatedly surfaced as a key dimension that was far more complex than just an external source of deadline pressure or an impetus for charter school organizers to move the process along. This variable affected decision making, relationships, and the overall feeling or "climate" of the group. It also defined the functioning of the organization as it progressed from stage to stage in its development. Butler's theory of organizational time provided a tool for analyzing the broader implications of time in the development of start-up charter schools in general. According to Butler:

> At the centre of the theory is the notion of a timeframe built around the interpretation and experience of events in the present, through knowledge derived from the past, while envisioning possible futures. In this sense, time is seen as a dependent variable, as an outcome of the organizational and institutional context within which a timeframe is located. Time is also seen to be an independent variable in the sense of enabling us to understand various organizational processes, in particular, those of decision making and learning.[12]

For example, during a charter school's developmental stage prior to petitioning the sponsor, there is ample time for a collective group to build community and envision the future of their school. The organizational experience changes when the group moves into actively petitioning for charter approval. Note the following excerpt from Community Charter's case study about the shift in the flavor or the ecology of the founding experience:

> The development phase prior to actively petitioning the sponsor—when the *ethos and values* of the school are

> forged—appears to be compatible with aspects of community building and grass roots organizing. There is time for an *organic solidarity* to develop through shared activities, brainstorming sessions, and communal events that include the children and extended family.[13] However, once formal negotiations are entered into with the sponsor and the community (i.e., local unions, neighborhood, and surrounding schools), the chartering experience shifts from a process characterized by a more voluntaristic pacing to one that is more controlled and directed by external rules and demands. Butler has coined the term *strategic time* to identify the organizational experience where the goal is to achieve an outcome in which a "move is followed by a counter move on the part of an opposition, and the next move has to await that counter move" (934). In this stage of the organization's development, parents and community members who come to the table with monetary resources, professional contacts, pertinent background knowledge, and/or skills in facilitating the work that must be done can create powerful positions for themselves.

D. J. Levinson's thesis on role theory in the organizational setting was utilized to further probe the experiences and the effects of parents in decision-making roles in a parent-run charter school.[14] Levinson's concept of role is not unitary, but multifaceted and relational. He formulates several distinct role concepts and suggests that an investigation of the relationships of these concepts, individual members, and other characteristics of an organization provides a method of understanding the nature and function of an organization. Some of the role-concepts that Levinson identifies that were important in this analysis are:

- *Role-demands.* These are external to the individual in the organization. They encompass the situational requirements and pressures of a given structural position, such as:

- *Role-facilities:* The means made available to individuals to fulfill organizational duties, such as technology, resources, and conditions of work; and
- *Role-dilemmas:* Contradictions experienced by individuals in their given positions, such as conflicting pressure between home life demands and school involvement.

- *Role-conception.* A rationale for one's position within the structure that is formed partially within the given organization and is influenced by personal background.
- *Role-performance.* Overt behavior of an individual in a given role or position that is the result of a number of forces, including role-demands, role-conception, and the situational context.

In studying the phenomenon of founding a parent-run charter school, one must take into consideration the state law, the local district and community, the backgrounds of the individuals participating in the process, and the means available to them (technology or "tools") for fulfilling their goal. As the schools evolve, the researcher's understanding of how the organizational climate functions for the individual members, how it influences interactions between members, and how those members and their interactions affect the functioning and stability of the organization is imperative. Note this next example from the Community Charter case study:

> The nuts-and-bolts interpretation of the mission may not, in its final form, exactly resemble what the founding members originally envisioned. This can cause conflict within a collective group if some members perceive that their individual voices are not being heard. Nevertheless, the necessity of moving ahead and getting systems in place for operations is paramount.
>
> The minimal "technological and ecological facilities" of Community Charter exacerbated these hurdles, inhibiting action and communication (175). Individuals

> were holding committee meetings in individual homes after work hours or on weekends; there was no equipment, such as copy and fax machines, for general use by the membership. Some of the members had access to technology and resources at their individual workplaces, allowing them to function more efficiently on behalf of the organization. Those who did not were unable to produce and contribute equally.

Moving on to the larger context of decentralization, I employed Blau and Scott's classificatory scheme based on *cui bono* ("who benefits?") to analyze the peculiarities of charter schools as de-regulated public institutions.[15] The four types of organizations Blau and Scott have identified are:

> - Mutual-benefit associations, where the prime beneficiary is the membership;
> - Business concerns, where the owners are the prime beneficiary;
> - Service organizations, where the client group is the prime beneficiary; and
> - Commonweal organizations, where the prime beneficiary is the public at large. (43)

Although parents in both case studies described their schools as "collectives" or "collective-like" organizations, firsthand observations revealed that work was rarely accomplished in a collective manner. As the organizations evolved, external factors and changes in the environment affected decision making, ideas about leadership, and the founding visions of the charters. The following excerpt from the C-Star case study provides an illustration:

> In both the first and second years, those individuals who assumed responsibility for the school's operations had to become knowledgeable about the intricacies and dilemmas the organization was facing. The experience of the parents serving on the second-year board reveals the role this knowledge played in affecting how they governed and their relationships with staff and other

> parents. As their understanding of charter funding and accountability developed (for example, the relationships of enrollment to financial stability and accountability to educational program), the parents on the board grew more conscious of the market-driven concerns—efficiency, survival, competition—of the organization... The critical intersection in charter schools of enrollment, educational program, and funding became visible to those serving in leadership positions in C-Star while remaining largely invisible to the majority of the parent body. This made it difficult—even for those members that argued strongly for the *mutual-benefit* model in the first year—not to adopt the attitude of *service organization* decision-makers ruling for clients who were ignorant of the big picture.

A longitudinal approach in the design of the study allowed the opportunity to observe the effects over time of parents joining, leaving, and/or assuming different roles within the organization and the impact of these changes on the initial educational visions and goals charted by the founders of the schools.

Data and reports from the U.S. Department of Education's four-year National Study of Charter Schools were used to situate the experiences of the two charter schools in the context of the state and national movements.

NOTES

1. Patty Yancey, "Parents as Partners in the Organization and Development of Charter Schools" (paper presented at the 1997 annual meeting of the American Educational Research Association, Chicago, IL) ERIC Document Reproduction Service No. Ps025479.

2. B. Latane, K. Williams, and S. Harkins, "Many Hands Make Light Work: The Cause and Consequences of Social Loafing," *Journal of Social Psychology 37* (1977): 822–32.

3. Frederick Erickson, "Qualitative Methods in Research on Teaching," in *Handbook of Research on Teaching*, ed. Merlin Wittrock (London: Collier-MacMillan, 1985), 119–69; Peter M. Blau and W. Richard Scott, *Formal Organizations: A Comparative Approach* (San Francisco: Chandler Publishing Company, 1962).

4. Matthew B. Miles and A. Michael Huberman, *Qualitative Data Analysis*, 2nd ed. (Thousand Oaks, CA: Sage Publications, 1994).

5. Richard Butler, "Time in Organizations: Its Experience, Explanations and Effects," *Organization Studies* 16.6 (1995): 925–50.

6. Daniel J. Levinson, "Roles, Personality, and Social Structure in the Organizational Setting," *Journal of Abnormal and Normal Social Psychology* 59 (1959): 170–80.

7. Blau and Scott, *Formal Organizations.*

8. Erickson, "Qualitative Methods."

9. Blau and Scott, *Formal Organizations*, 20.

10. Miles and Huberman, *Qualitative Data Analysis*, 113.

11. Ibid., 115.

12. Butler, "Time in Organizations," 925–26.

13. Butler, "Time in Organizations."

14. Levinson, "Roles, Personality, and Social Structure."

15. Blau and Scott, *Formal Organizations*.

CHAPTER THREE

BUT WE ALL LOVED THE IDEA

The chief owner and driver of the C-Star vision was Sara, a professional educator (European American) with an extensive track record in elementary teaching and teacher professional development, postsecondary teaching, and early childhood education research. With or without a charter law that would make it possible to start an alternative public school, Sara was determined to found her own elementary school in the local area:

> I knew by spring of '93 that I wanted to start another school somehow, and I went to my friend ... [who had a cooperative day care center] and asked, can I talk to your parents about if they would be interested in starting a school.... Out of that meeting and a couple of subsequent meetings where the rest of the cooperative community was informed of what was going on came about seven or eight parents who began working with me on founding the school ... Tina, who has been in my classroom observing ... found the charter law and I said, "No, no, that's just for schools that are already in existence." And

> she said, "No, here's a story about one in Santa Barbara. You can really do it from the ground up." And so— [1]

Sara had concrete experience in the founding of alternative schools and was clear about the educational program she wanted to implement. The provision for start-up schools in the California charter law answered Sara's concern about how to include ethnically diverse, low-income families in her school community. Less than a year after Sara decided to organize, C-Star's charter was approved.

When I arrived on-site in 1994, C-Star was just beginning its third month of operations. The hallways and classroom walls were shedding their Halloween and Dias de Los Muertos art, making way for winter projects and more renovation construction. The one-story school district building that houses the charter school sits unobtrusively on a quiet residential corner facing a large high school on one side and a park on the other. C-Star had negotiated a four-year lease on its space, which consisted of a portion of the main building, a fenced-in, asphalt area that served as the children's playground, and a 9′ x 12′ portable structure that C-Star planned to renovate and use in the future. The main building contained two classrooms, an art studio, an office, and a meeting room/lounge. At that time, the adjoining, vacant space in the main building was being renovated by the school district for other tenants.

The student population (44) in the fall of 1994 included a mix of high-, middle-, and low-income groups, with half of the youngsters qualifying for a free or reduced-price lunch. Kindergarten and first grade were the only grades offered that first year. There were 3 African American, 2 Chinese American, 3 Latino/a, 1 Native American, 2 Russian immigrant, 11 European American, and 22 mixed-race children. One quarter of the children were from single-parent households. There were 3 ESL students and 3 students from families where a language other than English was the primary one used in the household. As far as the staff, Sara (European American) was the full-time educational leader, first-grade teacher, and president of the C-Star nonprofit corporation; Yvonne (Chinese American) was the full-time kindergarten teacher; and Karla (Latina), was the half-time art teacher. One full-time parent volunteer/administrative assistant, Evelyn (European American), and a part-time student teacher, Lorraine (European American), comprised the remainder of the core staff. Parents volunteered as classroom teaching assistants, janitorial and office staff, and members of the C-Star board and committees.

Sara's Vision

Sara enjoyed talking about her educational philosophy so much that her enthusiasm was infectious. She would begin softly—the words coming very slowly and seriously—and rev up in volume and speed as she explained the C-Star vision:

> It [the educational program] was right there [She repeatedly jabs the air in front of her forehead.] ... Reggio, Sylvia Ashton-Warner, and Vivian Paley were my passions. They were—they come under a rubric I call hot cognition... And I think that's what the vision is. It is to take children where their interest and enthusiasm lie, and work with them—

An Italian philosophy and model of early childhood education called Reggio Emilia formed the foundation of Sara's program. The educational approach is named after a town in Northern Italy, where the idea was conceived and launched following World War II by educator Loris Malaguzzi. It is a unique system of public education that has combined arts and language in a "studio"environment for children under six years old, including infants and children with special needs. Reggio informs curriculum and pedagogy, organizational policy, relationships with parents and community, and the physical design of the environment.[2]

"Emergent curriculum" is the strategy that guides Reggio lesson planning. Teachers propose general educational objectives but do not establish in advance specific goals for each project and activity. They formulate hypotheses based on previous experience and adapt proposed objectives to the needs and interests of the children. Field trips are a core part of the curriculum, and the physical environment of the school is used as a tool for actively informing, documenting, and connecting the participants and their work. Parents are integrally involved in the life of Reggio schools.

The arts are considered a natural language or mode of expression of children in the Reggio philosophy, and art-making—visual and performing—occupies a central position in school life. Art-making and children's completed artwork are used by teachers as a noninvasive, dynamic form of assessment. The art teacher—known as the *atelierista* in Reggio schools—plays an integral role in the school; ensuring and providing the right conditions, expertise in craft, and knowledge of materials, as well as assisting teachers and administrators in identifying what is going on in the creative process and artwork of the child.

The language and literacy strands of Sara's core vision were Sylvia Ashton-Warner's early reading instruction and Vivian Gussin Paley's approach to creative storytelling. In the original C-Star charter petition, Sara described the two models:

> B. BEGINNING READING INSTRUCTION. The early reading approach of Sylvia Ashton-Warner expands logically into a Whole Language, Literature-Based language and literacy program... Ashton Warner's approach [is] based upon giving each child the particular words that matter to him or her [key vocabulary]...
>
> C. STORYPLAYING. This is the MacArthur prizewinning technique of children first dictating to the teacher and then directing [the stories] as plays with their classmates acting out the stories, as developed by Vivian Gussin Paley of the University of Chicago Laboratory School. Paley embodies the teacher-researcher, paying close attention to what the children in her classroom do and say and learning from that...
>
> Each of the [three] approaches supports the self-motivation, competence and interests of young children, and will enhance their dispositions to become lifelong

> learners. The approaches are particularly well-suited to children who are from homes under extra pressure due to poverty, illness or cultural marginalization, because they respect differences and encourage many modalities of expression.

Under "Program Outcomes" in the charter, more strategies and approaches are listed in the standards discussion:

> We expect children to improve measurably (1) in their approaches to new tasks, (2) in their interactions with others, both children and adults, and (3) in their ability to form and to test theories. Our program is designed to support children becoming literate and numerate, meeting the standards set in "Here They Come: Ready or Not!" and "It's Elementary" for language arts, mathematics, history-social sciences, science, health, education, and physical education, visual and performing arts and character education.[3]
>
> Primary teachers design investigative play activities as the way of teaching curriculum content, not as extras or enrichment activities outside the "real work" of the curriculum. Play is the vehicle through which curriculum is intelligently and thoughtfully learned, and, because the play always involves challenges to pupils' thinking, thinking becomes the method of learning.
>
> In the primary grades, play can and should occur in traditional creative/imaginative play activities using sand and water tables, clay blocks, Lego or other constructions, paint, "Wendy" houses, arts and crafts, scissors and paste, music, songs, and dance. It can and should occur as well in language learning, the learning of numbering and measuring, and learning about the world in which we live through sociological and scientific inquiries.
>
> Selma Wassermann
> Serious Players in the Primary Classroom[4]

Motivation of Parents and the Appeal of C-Star

The first parents recruited by Sara from the nursery co-op were primarily low to middle income and a mix of ethnicities: European American; African American; Latino/a; and interracial families (Asian American/European American and African American/European American). According to the founding parents who were still involved after operations began, the parent group was never particularly cohesive, even from the beginning. Parents would come to a flurry of meetings, disappear for a month or so, and then reappear. Norma, a European American mother who joined the group a couple of months after the initial group began meeting, recalled that "it was never clear who the group [charter school families] was until school started because people would pull in and out all the time." She explained her behavior and motivation:

> I would periodically just not show up for several months at a time and have no idea at all what was going on with [the planning process], but people would call and keep me informed.... In the meantime, of course, the more you become aware of how horrible the alternatives are [in the rest of the school district].... you [end up going] back to things you never would [have otherwise] ... The school [my child used to be] assigned to, her neighborhood school, you know ... they have duck and cover exercises ... There were drug runs through the—hey, she's not going to go to that school.

Like Norma, other parents were quite clear that their primary motivation to join Sara was their dislike of the local public schools. The "lack of any other alternative" was the number one reason reported by parents for their staying involved in the charter school group.

Sara believed that the main reason for the lack of a committed core of parents was a developmental process so lengthy (approximately 18 months) that "we didn't really have ground under our feet til four weeks before school opened." Founding parents speculated, however, that the key reason for the changing make-up of the founding group was that C-Star was Sara's vision, with the parents primarily participating as supporters, not partners.

Parents agreed that they were all drawn to the idea of being involved in a collective with other families focusing on a creative alternative school for their children.[5] Sara's educational vision appealed greatly to their personal philosophies about child rearing and schooling. One of the first members, Christina (a European American mother) explained how she first learned about the charter school and her initial attraction to the idea:

> [I was] a member of a parent participation co-op nursery school. I went to a co-op council meeting at one of the other nursery schools where Sara came to speak for two minutes because she was a friend or acquaintance of the—of the nursery school we were visiting.... She said that she was interested in accessing the parent participation people who were familiar with that kind of structure, because she wanted to start a school in [the local area]. And what she said there that struck me was ... "I don't know if this makes sense and I only have a few minutes to speak, but this school would be non-academic but intellectual." And that's instantly what attracted me, and I thought I'm very interested in—or not interested in—having my child fill out workbook exercises, but in actually having her mind—both of them—having their minds explore things. So I was very interested in it from the beginning.

Early planning meetings were held informally at Sara's home where parents could bring their children and browse through books and materials that outlined the educational theories and programs that comprised Sara's vision for the school. The proposed organizational structure verbalized by Sara was based on a collective or cooperative model with parents in primary decision-making roles. According to the involved parents, there was not much debate or rigorous discussion about the education program or the organizational structure among the members during this period. One mother characterized the quality of Sara's meetings/

workshops as "flakey, unfocused, and not very critical." According to Lorraine, the student teacher:

> The regular parent meetings were small then—I think only seven parents or so—and they were a combination of peer organizing, strategizing, envisioning, dealing with [the district].... The conversation mainly included collectively envisioning the new school.

Lorraine and Evelyn, a parent/volunteer administrative assistant at the charter school, believed that Sara did try to inform the parents about her plans, but that parents were not very interested in details and were willing to let Sara do the majority of the work. Evelyn exclaimed:

> People didn't only just trust Sara, they also let her do 90% of the work. They weren't really asking for a way to do more. Most were just tagging along.... But we all loved the, the idea of a parent collective, a parent cooperative school.

The parents were drawn to the idea of a parent-run charter school but were not clear about what this really meant. The ecology of these early planning meetings mirrored the casual, communal atmosphere that permeated alternative organizations such as the communes, collectives, free schools, and free clinics of the 1960s counterculture.[6] Meetings were described as "pretty loose," with children running about while parents talked with Sara informally. The flavor of these gatherings was attractive to most participants and appeared to fit their expectations of being a part of a "parent collective/coop type of organization."

She Was Only Doing Her Job

Among the local school board members, there was only one dissenting vote cast at the petition hearing against the C-Star charter. The reason stated for the one "no" vote was that the charter's educational program was too vague. The remaining school board members approved the C-Star charter on the condition that the group satisfy a list of requirements before opening. These included securing insurance; locating an appropriate site; providing more detail on assessment, governance and enrollment procedures; and drafting bylaws. The school board particularly noted that the charter petition lacked sufficient detail in the area of governance. The section of the petition devoted to C-Star's governance structure reads:

> The teachers, the artist, the pedagogue, if there is one, the parents, and 10 artists and other community people will govern the school. So, in the first year, with about 25 children, there will be a board of 25 parents, 1 teacher, 1 artist (on staff) and about 10 members of the community. In subsequent years parents may choose to have a smaller group represent them. Decisions will be made by consensus when possible, and by vote when consensus cannot be reached. Each family with a child in the school shall have one vote, as will each member of the teaching staff and each board member. There must never be enough community members and staff, separately or conjointly, to outvote the parents. That is, the parents, taken as a caucus, can veto any item. We believe that this sharing of power will ensure parental involvement. The parents and staff will write Bylaws to assure the smooth implementation of the Charter. There will be clear provision in the Bylaws for making necessary changes in the organization. The Bylaws will include a description of the relationship between staff, governing body and committees, and how each group is selected. The school will not open until the Bylaws are established.

Because the school board was particularly concerned about the governance system of the charter school, Sara enlisted the aid of some pro bono lawyers to advise her on the drafting of the bylaws. During their discussions, the lawyers advised Sara to adopt a more traditional nonprofit corporate structure for two reasons: to satisfy school board concerns and to facilitate C-Star's 501(c)3 application process. These issues were high on Sara's list of concerns; she did not want to risk the opening of the school being delayed by the school board and the quicker the 501(c)3 status was approved, the better their chances were for securing outside funding. The solution appeared logical and Sara pushed ahead for the change. Some key points outlined in the new bylaws included:

- The authorized number of directors of the corporation shall be seven (7) until changed by an amendment of the Articles of Incorporation or these Bylaws amending this Section 2 duly adopted by the members. The Board of Directors of this Corporation shall at all times consist of one (1) employee of the Corporation, and a majority of the remaining directors shall at all times consist of Parents who are members of this Corporation.

- The Chairperson of the Board (if there is such an officer appointed) shall, when present, preside at all meetings of the Board of Directors and shall perform all the duties commonly incident to that office. The Chairperson of the Board shall have the authority to execute in the name of the corporation all bonds, contracts, deeds, leases, and other written instruments to be executed by the corporation (except where by law the signature of the President is required)...

- Subject to such supervisory powers, if any, as may be given by the Board of Directors to the Chairperson of the Board, the President shall be the general manager and chief executive officer of the corporation and shall perform all duties commonly incident to that office. The President shall preside at all meetings of the members and, in the absence of the Chairperson of the Board, or, if there is none, at all meetings of the Board of Directors, and shall perform such other duties as the Board of Directors may from time to time determine.

One father, who was asked to participate on the bylaw committee, expressed his reservations to his wife about this major change in the organization. After a meeting with the lawyers in which Sara was appointed President of the Corporation, he was particularly upset. Christina recalled:

> Derrick [her husband] actually had expressed some serious concerns about being involved with [C-Star] because he did feel that Sara had not been up front as to what the hierarchical situation was and how that was to be. And I said you know it's a good school—if she needs to, you know, be president, why don't we just let her be, and I kind of just blew it off until it actually occurred to me that it was more important than that—

Most of the parents paid little attention to this change and accepted Sara's explanation that C-Star's organizational structure would still be run "like a collective." Norma, one of the few parents who was upset by the bylaws, described the long phone conversation she had with Sara about the change in governance:

> Once they granted us a charter... Sara was pushing people that we had to—in order to be incorporated, we had to—have officers and we had to have bylaws. So with about five days notice I was told that there was going to be a meeting about approving the bylaws and electing the officers. I was like, well, who are these people and where are the bylaws? I mean can't we read them ahead of time? ...I actually managed to get a set of the bylaws about a day before the meeting with a lot of trouble—really not easy to—I finally got them and came to this meeting.... I had some specific concrete things that I wanted to put my two cents in about the bylaws... I mean I've been involved in a few organizations in my time, and I've been involved in helping to write bylaws a few places, and these were nonsense. These were awful, these were some kind of corporate bylaws.... Before I came to the meeting I had called Sara and said I didn't understand where these particular bylaws came from. I

> understood we were trying to create a co-op type organization. At which point that's when she corrected me and said no, in fact, we were not going to have a co-op—That was the first to my knowledge—Anyway she [Sara] would say things like, you know, we—The most important thing we have to do here is we have to get moving. We've got to be incorporated or we can't go back to the school board and get a building and whatever else was dependent on it, and this democratic process is standing in our way right now.

Norma was not satisfied with Sara's explanation, withdrew from the group, and resumed looking elsewhere for an alternative school for her daughter. Norma's protest, however, was just a ripple in a large, tranquil pond. The majority of parents were willing to abandon "this democratic process" to move things along. Bobbi, an African American mother, explained her willingness to just let things happen:

> There are many mistakes I think that have been made along the way in terms of jumping into something without really knowing what was there. And I think for me the, the main reason is that it seemed like the best alternative of all my alternatives and I didn't want it to be terrible. I wanted it to be good.

The Site

At the same time, negotiations with the school district about a charter school site were underway. The school board required C-Star to locate operations in one of the vacant school district buildings, but there was no procedure in place for facilitating this process. Negotiations were described by both Sara and Karla (the first teacher hired; Latina) as "monstrous." Karla, who "didn't expect to be negotiating leases" as a part of her job, recalled that working with the school district on this matter was "one series of disappointments after another." Karla's stories about site negotiations corroborated further the chaotic character of the founding process resulting from the lack of guidelines from the district. She shook her head and sighed often when telling the story:

> The guy who was representing the school district… He did at least talk to me. He wouldn't even talk to Sara after a while. He wouldn't have anything to do with Sara. He told her off in a meeting and then never spoke to her again—and we needed to talk to somebody…. He [messed up] the lease, signed on paper, and then later, came back two weeks later said that won't work and… then we weren't supposed to be paying rent and we ended up paying rent—

Two district staff workers recalled their own frustrations dealing with the charter school during this time:

> No one thought they [C-Star] would get it off the ground. They had so many questions and they—it was one thing, one thing and then another and another and another and—

> [Those in charge at the school district] didn't want us to spend a lot of time—didn't want us to waste too much time figuring … out [how to help C-Star] … No one seemed to like them [the charter school] and I think—yeah—you know, they were a pain—

The location of the site was still up in the air one month before the school doors were scheduled to open. Parents were actively inquiring into enrolling in other schools when the district gave Sara the keys to a building that was in need of major repair and located in a residential area far from the neighborhoods of most of the C-Star families and staff. The structure was "a construction nightmare" that needed asbestos removal, replacement of windows, and serious plumbing and electrical work. Sara was told by the district rep, "It's this location or none."

With no money for start-up or capital improvements, parent skills and volunteer labor were the only resources available to carry out the necessary renovations. Although the task was daunting, the finalization of a site signaled to the parents that "the school was really going to happen." The parents rallied and turned out in force to help. Those parents with construction experience—carpenters, plumbers, painters, electricians, and masons—who had previously remained on the periphery of the founding process, moved into central roles in the organization. Others participated in vital support roles, such as making breakfast and lunch for the workers, scrounging at flea markets for furniture and supplies, sewing, cleaning, and hauling and dumping debris.

The physical and inclusive nature of the work appeared to trigger and/or revitalize the emotional bonds and shared goals of all the families. Norma, who rejoined the group during this time, visibly brightened when describing the scene:

> I actually got fired up with enthusiasm. People were painting, creating the space, and that was exciting.... That was really exciting, to have kids hanging out while their parents were all working. There was no way that you wouldn't get enthused about this.

Norma's recollection characterized the feelings other C-Star parents expressed in their stories about the renovation. "Energizing," "renewal," and "the real beginning" were words and phrases that captured the sentiments of those involved then. Joining together and physically transforming the dark, dank, shabby facility into a bright, colorful learning space for their kids reawakened the parents' sense of membership and reaffirmed their connection to the group. The nature of the work allowed everyone to take part, feel necessary, and play a role in the founding process. Durkheim's theory of "collective effervescence" comes to mind—the group euphoria resulting from communal celebrations or collective rituals such as the barn-raising events of rural, agricultural communities.[7] In contrast to the sometimes isolating routine of everyday life, the collective tackling of the renovation work dissolved differences between individuals, energized the group, and satisfied a fundamental need to belong, to be connected to one another, and to share a set of norms that offer direction and meaning.[8]

Because of this incredible mobilization of the parents, the school opened on schedule. The art studio and offices were still partially under construction and not fully functional, but the spacious classrooms were brightly painted, creatively decorated, and filled with sunlight for the 44 kindergartners and first graders who streamed in on the first day of school.

The Pendulum Swings

For the proposed educational program in the first year of operations, three teachers were needed for the kindergarten and first-grade classrooms and art studio. Because of a tight budget, Sara reluctantly agreed to serve as the school director, as well as the first grade teacher. She hired Karla, the art teacher, with little difficulty in February of 1994; however, the search for the kindergarten teacher (Yvonne) went "down to the wire." Sara found both applicants via word of mouth. A personnel committee of parents interviewed the teachers after Sara recommended them for hire.

Because Karla was known throughout the community as an accomplished professional artist and arts educator, Sara and the personnel committee moved quickly to hire her. Yvonne's prior teaching experience was not extensive and was limited to working with preschool ages, so there was more debate about hiring her.

Yvonne had found out about the C-Star job opening after attending one of Sara's independent, professional development workshops for teachers in the local community. She was well aware of her inexperience but applied anyway, believing that she could "learn from Sara" while working on the job. She admired Sara as an educator and was honored that Sara wanted her for the position.

Sara believed that she could successfully mentor Yvonne, but Karla adamantly disagreed. There was some discussion among the personnel committee, but Sara's strong recommendation coupled with the fact that school was opening in a matter of weeks carried the decision. Karla and one of the hiring committee members made an attempt to advertise for other candidates, but the move failed and Yvonne was hired two days after C-Star received the keys to their building.

Of the three paid C-Star employees, only Karla requested a written contract and job description. In the drafting of these documents for Karla, Sara failed to specify the organizational or decision-making structure of the staff. In addition, the documents did not clarify whether Karla's preoperational planning hours would be volunteer or paid time, and there were differing opinions about what had been agreed to in verbal discussions.

Karla had agreed to work at C-Star assuming that decisions would be made collectively and that she would be paid for her planning time. She believed that she had received a verbal commitment from Sara to pay her for this planning time. Sara did not recall promising payment of these hours and complained that she had "volunteered numerous hours in setting up the school and was not expecting payment." Karla brought up the issue of payment again when a foundation grant was secured that summer. Karla submitted an invoice for six to ten hours per week from March to July to the treasurer of the C-Star board of directors. By mid-year in the first year of operations, the board had still not conveyed their decision to Karla.

As far as the absence of details clarifying the hierarchical structure of the staff, Sara explained that "it seemed so obvious" that Karla would report to her that she did not specifically indicate it in the job description or the contract:

> Her commitment to learn from me was so clearly voiced that it never occurred to me that she would think she was at the same level in the power structure as I was.

These oversights appear to be glaringly obvious omissions for a professional educator as experienced as Sara. However, it appears that Sara's passionate belief and commitment to her educational vision obscured the potential danger of internal conflict resulting from inattention to detail in such matters as personnel contracts and job descriptions.[9] Sara was very self-assured about the innovativeness and cutting-edge quality of her proposed educational program and had been looking for a way to start another school for ten years. She referred often to the combination of Reggio

Emilia, Paley, and Ashton-Warner models that formed the foundation of the C-Star program as her "passions" and assumed that Karla shared her enthusiasm and commitment to the C-Star vision equally. The two educators did appear to share the educational philosophies that underlie the C-Star program, but they differed greatly in their opinions about what it meant to work at C-Star. Sara was willing to forego monetary compensation because the school was "her dream." Karla, although intrigued by the innovative educational potential of C-Star, viewed her position at the charter school as a job, not a calling. She assumed that she would be paid for her work during the planning stage, an assumption that Sara could not understand given the lack of start-up funds available to C-Star. There were also mountains of other details that Sara was attending to simultaneously, creating a situation where sufficient time was not available to think through individual decisions thoroughly.

Richard Butler explains that this is not an uncommon experience for top decision-makers faced with a highly irregular period in an organization's development. "A probabilistic coming together of problems and solutions" is one of the ways that decisions are made when there is a lack of clearly defined guidelines or policies to follow.[10] Karla appeared on the horizon at the same time that Sara was in need of someone with the necessary skills, experience, and qualifications to fill a key position in the organization. Sara leapt at the chance to get Karla on the team and rushed through the interviewing and hiring details.

Because of her years of experience and status in the community, Karla expected to operate within the organization's *social structure* as Sara's equal.[11] Karla agreed that she could learn a lot from Sara, but she also believed that Sara could gain critical knowledge about the arts from working with her. She argued emphatically that she "would never have accepted the position" if she had known that she would be supervised by Sara. Although Sara believed herself to be in charge—at the top of the power structure—Karla was not receptive to this idea. Karla was also not willing to "let it slide" and concede to Sara's authority.

Yvonne, on the other hand, was very willing to work on a lower level of the hierarchy, approaching her position as an opportunity to learn. She wanted direction and mentoring, but Sara was juggling teaching and administrative duties and had little time for mentoring. Coming on board just weeks before the opening of the school, Yvonne had little time to learn about the peculiarities of the organization or her position/role within the structure. On the first day of school, she was very hesitant in her manner with the children and the parents, and Karla and Sara were barely on speaking terms. The C-Star staff launched the first year of operations as a disaggregated group lacking the "tools" to collaborate, support each other, or assure parents through the most difficult stage of a start-up charter school.

I Thought It Would Be Different

Six days after school opened, Madge—a kindergarten parent volunteering in her child's classroom—approached Sara about what she perceived as "a lack of a curriculum plan and no teacher control" in the K-classroom. Sara was in no mood for such feedback at this time and as Bobbi, a first grade parent, recalled:

> We were all so drained from the physical and emotional task of reconstructing the space—Sara especially. It was much too early to criticize [anything]…. We figured it would blow over—

Madge did not drop the issue and drafted a memo for the board of directors and the parent membership that began:

> To the Board of Directors and the Members of the [C-Star] School:
>
> I have spoken with several members of the school, and believe as a result of those discussions and my own observations that the current structure of the kindergarten and first grade classes is not effective. If this experiment in education is to succeed, we must act immediately to make better use of our assets and compensate for our weaknesses. In the memorandum which follows, I

will describe (1) what problems I believe we are experiencing in our classrooms, (2) one method for corroborating the existence of any problems, (3) a proposed solution involving restructuring the classrooms. Following distribution of this memorandum, a meeting will be set to discuss these issues before the Board. I hope that all the interested members of the school will attend and participate in that meeting.

1. The Problems Appearing in Our Classrooms

I have identified several areas of concern through my observations of the kindergarten room and statements made to me by other parents. First, there is a feeling that not much of substance is happening in the classrooms. There appears [sic] to be insufficient materials for use by all the children and those materials that are presented are not sufficiently varied from day to day. Basically, the same rather "thin" projects are set out every day.

Second, the teachers have both strengths and weaknesses that have been immediately apparent. [Sara] is quite good at leading the first grade group activities and in keeping a high level of energy and activity going in that classroom. However, many first grade parents feel that [Sara's] individual interaction with the children has not been satisfactory. On the other hand, every kindergarten parent I have spoken with agrees that [Yvonne] has excellent one-on-one skills with the children and that she does very well in getting the children to interact with her in small groups. But she has not been successful in working with the whole class in large group activities.

Third, the special teaching methods set forth in the charter have not been implemented. We parents understand it is too early to expect full implementation of those plans.

> 2. Do These Problems Really Exist?
>
> It has been [Sara's] stated position that the problems described above do not exist, that both classrooms are operating at an adequate base-line level, and that nothing better can be expected by the parents at this time. If there are doubts among the Board members and/or the school members about how things are going, I propose that both classrooms be evaluated immediately by parents and staff. Because some parents are uncomfortable expressing their opinions directly to the staff or speaking up publicly, the evaluations could be anonymous. The evaluation should cover the factors described above: the effectiveness of the classrooms/materials and the skills displayed or found lacking in the teachers ...

The memo continued for another page, describing problems and offering solutions. Sara drafted a two-page response to Madge's memo:

> I appreciate the time and energy [Madge] has put into the school and find her thinking stimulates mine. I agree, generally, with some of the ideas [Madge] presents, and disagree with others. I will discuss the memo in the same order it was written.
>
> 1. The goals in any good early childhood room during the first few days (we have just completed day 8) should be to make children feel at home. Children need a place to be familiar, they need to know that things have places, that they happen in orderly ways....
>
> I am unable to reply to the general criticism [Madge] reports about my individual interactions with the children. I would have to hear them from people who had concerns, and I would listen very carefully. I'm sure in my recent exhaustion that I have made errors—but nobody has asked me to clear up any of them with their

> children at this time. I agree that Yvonne has excellent one-on-one skills, and I agree in principle that we should be working with the children in overlapping ways. I am not sure that the time is ready for that yet....
>
> I think we need a problem-solving perspective in the school, and mostly I feel [Madge's] letter brings that to bear. I am not ready for her to decide a timetable for the staff and the children, but am ready to work with the whole community, as my energy returns, to build the school strongly and well. Can we return to this discussion mid-October, after the children and staff have come to know each other a little bit?

Sara also asked other parents to submit written statements refuting the complaining mother's concerns. Madge then tried to take her concerns to the C-Star board of directors but found there to be no grievance process in place. The public comment period designated for the beginning of all board meetings—10 minutes, up to five speakers at 2 minutes each—was frustratingly brief for Madge, and she began to feel that she was being stonewalled by Sara. The incident escalated into a bitter tug-of-war and resulted in Madge pulling her child out of the school by October.

Although the kindergarten complaints eased after Madge's exit, concerns about the charter school's curriculum and discipline policy continued "underground" among a small group of parents. The most common criticisms that circulated among parents about the curriculum were:

> Why don't we have long-term projects like we were promised? I thought we were going to have a lot of those. And what about field trips? I thought we were going to have a lot of those.
>
> The classroom learning doesn't reflect Reggio. Our classrooms are supposed to be inspired by the philosophy of Reggio. I haven't seen it.

> This curriculum is just not working. It's—it's too soft. The story play stuff is too—too loose—the kids are just playing around ... more structure, yeah, more structure. And I want math more than once a week and homework.

Sara felt strongly that the parents who were complaining did not understand the education program because it was such a radical alternative to traditional public school practice. Yvonne thought the parents were too impatient and wanted everything to be "instantly perfect":

> I thought when I came to this school—I thought it would be different. I thought we were going to try to develop a curriculum—a way of teaching and learning that was different.... No one wants to [allow for] time to grow and develop. This environment is so—it takes a lot out of me. It's so hard. There's a lot of judgment and criticism, so quickly. We're just beginning—we need time to grow.

As far as discipline, some parents believed that Sara was too strict and harsh; others believed that she was not strict enough. Some parents did not want their children placed in "time out" for misbehavior because it was "humiliating." Others felt that children who were "unruly" needed to be disciplined and that "time out" was too lenient a strategy. This issue grew to be the most contentious and problematic of all the parent criticisms leveled at Sara. The following parent quotes recorded at meetings illustrate the range of opinions about discipline and Sara's performance as a teacher.

> I think it has to be ... twofold. I think you have to spell out requirements and a code of conduct for the teacher, but I think you also have to spell out the code of conduct for the children. Both of them [need] to be held responsible—and if the children can't deal with it then the parents have to be held responsible because if you want a teacher to respect the child, the child also has to respect the teacher. And if the child can't do that then

the parent has to be brought in.... Now I'm gettin' kind of sick an' tired of having everything brought down where children in this school bring the level of education down because of discipline problems. My child suffers as a result of this and I'm getting awful tired of it.

Our children need to be treated with dignity and those issues aren't always necessarily discipline problems, you know. I mean just a child being acknowledged or a child being ignored. There's a need for all the children to be treated with dignity—and I feel like that happens sometimes and sometimes it doesn't.

Discipline is a really interesting word, and I think one that for a lot of people brings up automatically, they think—You hear the word discipline and the next word that comes out of your mouth is, means some sort of punishment. And this isn't the best dictionary definition, but I was wanting to read that because I thought that it was—it's important for us.... I'm hoping that there is a lot of discipline going on in schools, and I certainly don't mean a whack upside the head.... [Our job is] to help children develop self-control, and I think we do need to come up with a system that enables children to do that. And also recognize that it's not innate. That it's a process that humankind is still trying to figure out how to do after thousands of years of being around and I really ... I agree with people that there needs to be some sort of balance and boundaries set, because I can see where the children who are having a very difficult time working that out suck up a lot of the adults' energy in the classroom.

Yeah, we need to establish consequences, but we also need to define, define behavior positively and consistently. No yelling, you [Sara] shouldn't yell at them. You're too loud. They should resolve and talk about issues with each other without an adult saying, "Say

> you're sorry." Of course the adult should be right there for support and comfort ... but you shouldn't yell.

Board elections were coming up in October and some of the disgruntled parents decided to run for seats. Sara's support was still quite solid among the parent membership and most of the board members, initially appointed by Sara, retained their seats. The board was composed of Sara, six parents (African American, four European Americans, Japanese American) and one outside community member (African American).[12] The outside community member was a trusted family friend and colleague of Sara's and rarely attended meetings, often voting by proxy through her. As a result of the election, only one parent "who was not considered in Sara's camp" won a board seat.

The election was viewed as a victory by Sara and evidence that her performance was satisfactory among the majority of parents. Nevertheless, a small, vocal group headed by Norma and Christina continued their standoff with Sara and kept lobbying the board about "getting on the agenda" for a substantial amount of time in order to sufficiently air their grievances. From their perspective, the board appeared unwilling to hear their criticisms and was unresponsive to their concerns. According to the board chairperson, however, the board of directors appointed a committee to research and set up a grievance process, and the parents who were delegated this task never followed through. By December, a formal grievance process had still not been established and the disgruntled parents were extremely frustrated. Christina recalled, "That's when I began to wonder if we had been had."

Sara's supporters and neutral parents were in the majority during the first semester of school, but those who opposed her were far more vocal and adamant about their opinions. The staff continued to focus separately on their own pressing issues: Yvonne, struggling to maintain control of her classroom; Karla, appealing to the board about revisiting the hierarchical structure of the staff; and Sara, appealing privately to her allies among the parent body to support her and the educational program. As questions and concerns lingered unresolved through the first semester without board resolution, the dissension began to spread. Sara's supporters grew increasingly unhappy about the polarization of the group and wanted the issues to be settled. With energies focused on the classroom, the board of directors and Sara found it difficult to mobilize themselves and other C-Star members to set up a legitimate grievance process that would be acceptable to all factions. Sara, emotionally and physically exhausted from the planning and preparation phases, became frustrated with the parents' lack of patience and unwillingness to leave the staff alone to "do their job." Her manner toward parents and students appeared brusque and ill-tempered. By December, parents were meeting secretly at each other's homes to talk about Sara's role as leader of the organization.

Why All the Fuss?

The fact that a formal grievance procedure had not been established before the school opened for business allowed minor complaints to fester and then resurface at a later date as major problems. It is interesting to note that serious, concrete opposition by parents on governance and structural issues did not occur until the children actually started attending the school. Although the parents had questions and concerns during the planning stage, it was not until they perceived a problem in the day-to-day education of their children that they sought to exercise their power.

The C-Star membership believed strongly that they shared a "collective vision" for educating their children, but it became obvious after operations began that the alternative educational ideas that parents and staff held individually, while theoretically similar, were vastly different in reality. The curriculum philosophy that Sara proposed for the school emphasizes "emergent curriculum," which means that teachers propose general educational objectives but do not establish in advance specific goals for each project and activity. The parents loved the idea, but in actually observing this process in the classrooms, they were disturbed by the lack of academic structure and began to ask, "What IS the plan here?"

Sara, when she was recruiting parents, had explained that the school would be "nonacademic, but intellectual." She held workshops early in the planning process on the three proposed curriculum strands—Reggio Emilia, Sylvia Ashton-Warner, and Vivian Paley—but these sessions, according to some parents, were not rigorous and did not continue and develop into serious discussions. According to Nicholls, it is critical that teachers working together "be prepared to discuss the meaning of the ideas and principles underlying their innovations in order to establish, among other things, that they are at least talking about the same thing."[13] In the case of charter schools, it is crucial that these discussions include parents and allow for their input and criticisms.[14]

A school's curriculum and classroom discipline do not appear to have anything to do with organizational structure or governance; but, as pointed out earlier, the conflicts at C-Star over structure and governance emerged because of the parents' concerns about classroom curriculum and procedures. It is important for charter school organizers to realize, especially in working with groups that combine a variety of cultures, races, and socioeconomic classes, that terms such as "classroom discipline" and "intellectually challenging" can have vastly different meanings. Being aware that there are many different, heartfelt perspectives on what "a good education" entails should motivate organizers to seriously address the issues of ongoing parent education and the establishment of grievance procedures and policies for airing concerns. C-Star's board of directors found it to be hard, after operations began, to move quickly enough to set up a process to deal with all the grievances. If a structure had been in place, it would have possibly allowed those parents who were most critical to gain confidence in the organizational system and separate it from their dislike and mistrust of Sara.[15]

According to Swidler, organizing collectively, although "it is the goal of virtually all alternative organizations," is extremely difficult and unstable.[16] Often one of the main reasons that people are drawn to participate in the organization of alternative schools is "out of attraction or devotion to dynamic, engaging personalities."[17] The C-Star community might not characterize themselves as being devoted to Sara because of her engaging personality, but they were aware that her drive and tenacity were key elements in starting the school.

The nature of the charter school founding process is chaotic and highly novel, with many concurrent events impinging on the opening of a school. This type of work often aligns with a particular type of leader who can deal with chaos and uncharted territory. Because of the lack of rules and guidelines that articulate policies and procedures, charter founding fits hand in glove with the leadership style of a "charismatic" authority. The "charismatic" leader offers the highly ambiguous organization "a way of reducing the duration of a decision" by taking hold of a situation and driving matters forward.[18]

Collective organizing or democratic decision making can become burdensome when time is precious. The hours spent deliberating in meetings can be endless and may appear to some participants to be holding up the real work that needs to be done. The parents were more than willing, during the preoperations stage, to allow Sara free rein in establishing the operational framework, and they trusted her to provide them with the school of their choice.

For Sara, in taking control, she was only doing her job. She was very cognizant of the fact that it was imperative to push things through on her own in order to meet the fall deadline of opening the school. Lorraine, who worked closely with her in the classroom, said that Sara felt responsible for those parents who had remained with her through the long, difficult planning process. Lorraine added that Sara believed that she would fail the parents if the school did not open that particular fall.

Neither the parents nor Sara completely understood the full import of the foundation that was being laid. How the rules and goals of the larger structure determine relationships and affect everyday decision making was invisible to the parents at this stage of the organization's development. A prime example was the founding group's approach to establishing the governance system. The majority viewed the drafting of the bylaws as a formality to appease the school board—just another bureaucratic hurdle to be cleared out of the many roadblocks to their goal.[19]

By not clarifying information or asking questions, by allowing one member or a few to take on the responsibilities of the group, and by shrugging off decisions that were critical to the organization, the C-Star parents essentially turned over control to Sara.

This kind of acquiescent behavior became so much a part of the C-Star *social process* that it was accepted as just a part of life in the organization.[20] Sara's *role-conception* and *role-performance* as leader fostered this behavior among the parents.[21] As the professional educator of the group she viewed herself as the most appropriate person to be in charge of setting up operational policies and systems. She possessed the necessary tools and knowledge to meet the *role-demands* of starting a school from scratch; therefore, it did not seem important to her to slow the process down by soliciting parental input and involvement.[22]

In hindsight, founding parents recalled that they complained to each other before the school opened about Sara's "aggressiveness and tendency to railroad," but they acknowledged that her persistence and tenacity were necessary traits for pushing the charter process forward. Sara's determination was definitely recognized as relentless, even in the surrounding local community, in her quest to open the school. During an informal interview with a school board member, he described Sara's "do-or-die" manner in getting the charter approved:

> Oh I remember her! She was everywhere, oh God, everywhere! She camped on our doorstep one day—all day—until I finally came out of the house to talk to her. I had to come out—she wouldn't leave. Oh—oh—[laughing] I would have voted for the charter school just so she would leave me alone.

Second Semester

After winter break, the following letter signed by 11 parents was delivered to Sara:

> A group of first grade parents have met to discuss some very serious concerns we have. Those concerns center on the following issues:
>
> 1. What we have observed as unacceptable behavior by you, Sara, in the classroom toward both children and adults;

> 2. The lack of a written curriculum with both short and long term objectives;
> 3. Your resistance to parental involvement and ideas.
>
> We will discuss these issues at the [next] parent meeting... and plan to work to resolve these issues with you.

The next parent meeting dissolved in tears and harsh words and polarized the community even further. As a result, five parents drafted another memo demanding the immediate resignation of Sara "from the Board of Directors and as the principal and first grade teacher at the school." The memo outlined the following reasons for their action:

a. Regarding Sara's performance as a teacher:
   - repeated instances of abusive and disrespectful language and punitive disciplinary methods in the classroom
   - lack of substantive, acceptable curriculum
   - repeated refusal to work with parents to establish positive behavior guidelines

b. Regarding Sara's performance as a leader:
   - lack of administrative abilities and failure to train and/or work with staff in a supportive manner
   - the employment of divisive tactics encouraging the formation of factions, rather than building consensus and unity
   - the loss of the confidence of the C-Star community

The memorandum ended with an encouragement of "all parents to participate in these difficult discussions" and an assurance that the persons responsible for the memorandum were "not interested in creating a chaotic classroom arena where individual parents will be changing the curriculum at whim, but want to find a leader who can articulate and implement an educational program which we can all support." After the circulation of this last memo it was decided, at the suggestion of a "neutral" parent, that further meetings were in need of mediation.

A special meeting was called and 25 parents, all 5 staff members (paid and volunteer) and 2 mediators were in attendance. During Sara's report to the group, she relayed an incident "with the blocks" that had occurred that same day in the first grade classroom. I did not witness the block incident firsthand and learned of it through the testimonies in meetings. Sitting in a rocking chair with her hands clasped in her lap, Sara began her report in a quiet voice:

> I had a very busy week, very stressful. One mom has reported that her child is feeling the struggle and stress of us adults. I am worried about that, but I have kept my commitments. I have started writing in a journal and I have read the reports that parents wrote and I found them straight. This week has been hard.... I've gone to the doctor and he's asked me to cut my work time down to 20 hours a week for one month. This made me think of [Karla's] request for her job to be finite and I realize I need a finite job, too. Today the children were playing in the block room and I told them to clean up. The children said no. [Gregory, a parent volunteer] was supervising in the block room and so I left it with him. Later I came into the block room again from my classroom and told the children to clean up and put the blocks away. I returned to the block room again. Nothing had been done. I come back again after working in the classroom with some other children and then I come back again and I see that there is absolutely no progress being made toward cleaning up—I then knocked down the blocks in a manner that some characterize as "pretty dramatic" or "explosive." [Her shoulders slump.] I shouldn't have done it. I lost patience. I was tired.

After Sara finished, Gregory—the parent volunteer who was in the first-grade classroom at the time of the incident—spoke up:

> I want to add to Sara's block story—it was like a tornado when she pushed those blocks down. Two girls cried. I was flabbergasted.... She asked me to do something. I was doing it my—uh, okay, maybe not fast enough—but it undermined my authority as a parent in the classroom. I apologized, tried to work it out with the two girls. The boys had already left. We have to continue to work on this.

Some parents were horrified by Sara knocking down the blocks. Others could not figure out why there was so much concern about such a trivial incident. The following week another meeting was held and the discussion about the block incident continued. The debate went back and forth:

> Mother A: Yeah ... I'm a volunteer here, I've been coming here once a week since September and I—in the beginning of September there were two boys who were discipline problems. They used to play with one another especially, and instead of forcing them apart or disciplining them, [Sara] talked to them and she talked them through ways to work with one another ... and I've seen her do that continuously and from my—from my viewpoint I've never seen her abuse a child. I've never seen her ... physically or emotionally abuse a child and it surprises me that there are so many objections. I've only seen her try to teach the kids how to deal with situations on their own and she's given them a lot of freedom.
>
> Father: You think they respect her?
>
> Mother A: I think they do, until the last few weeks. I've seen a couple of incidents.... I can see that students are just saying NO, and there's nothing that can be done about it. I mean up

until now both [Lorraine] and [Sara] they've worked really hard at establishing authority here—and the kids, they get the kids to do things. Even when they don't want to with anyone else. And like today—I saw a situation where two students didn't wanna do anything—didn't want to do what the rest of the class was doing and instead of fighting it [Sara] let it go.... and I don't like this because we can't fight—I mean if the kids now don't want to do something they have so much power. It's really upsetting.

[Cross talk. Mediators restore order.]

Mother B: I've been very supportive of Sara but I do have that concern of safety. The block—a block can be very dangerous, and in that way it's—it's scary to me what could happen. Maybe she does need some—some ease in the job. Maybe it is too much and maybe we could bring in a teacher—a teacher to help in the afternoons if [turns toward Sara] your hours do need to be reduced for a month.

[More cross talk. Several parents voice concerns.]

Sara: There is just one more detail that I would like to be heard if you will, and that is that I very carefully put my body between the children and the blocks and pushed them away. There was never, and I want you [looking at Mother B] to know. This is very important to me. There was never an attempt to throw blocks at children.

Mother B: Uh, oh, I didn't mean that you meant to do it. The fact that it could happen. It does upset me.

At the end of this meeting, with the mediators' guidance, a committee was formed to begin researching how schools similar to C-Star deal with discipline in the classroom. Sara was also asked to draft a discipline policy for review. A "Think Tank" of parents was also established to brainstorm and submit suggestions about how to modify the organizational structure of the charter school. Other parent volunteers were tapped to organize a C-Star community-wide meeting focusing on curriculum development. This work, however, did not seem to ease the dissension, and by the second week of March, neither the C-Star board nor the parent community had made any major decisions. Sara was taking Fridays off from the classroom, by order of her doctor, due to "extreme stress and fatigue."

In March, an incident occurred in the first grade classroom in which Sara restrained an African American boy (Terrence) from hitting a white boy (Elliot). Norma and another parent who were volunteering in the classroom found Sara's actions overly harsh and aggressive and decided that a call must be made to Terrence's parents. Lorraine, the student teacher who witnessed the incident, was shocked by the parents' reactions to the incident:

> I was struck—struck! by the way Norma and [the other parent volunteer] saw the whole thing. Terrence is not a violent boy and even though I wasn't sure if he was going to pound Elliot—BUT his movements toward Elliot were aggressive. Sara took his hand—did not force him or pull him, and took him and held him on her lap. Sara was not abusive. It's disturbing to me that they would think so.

A week or so after this incident, Norma, Christina, Derrick, and another C-Star parent contacted the president of the district school board, C-Star's sponsor, and asked to meet with him to discuss their concerns about the charter school. In the meeting, they complained of Sara's discipline strategies in the classroom and her performance as the educational leader, and they speculated about the future of the school if Sara were removed as director. The school board president was most concerned with their complaints about the disciplinary tactics and followed up the meeting with a consultation with school district staff and a phone call to Karla.

Within days the school district placed Sara on administrative leave with pay while officials investigated allegations that she had verbally and physically abused several children. At a parent meeting that took place right after the news circulated throughout the C-Star community, the kindergarten room was overflowing with parents, most of whom were visibly angry and confused. The mediators asked at the beginning of the meeting who wanted to speak. As members raised their hands, the mediators wrote their names down on the board. Facilitation was difficult because of the high level of emotion.

> Parent L: The board needs to talk to us and tell us what happened. We were told in the letter that the board would notify us about what happened … I think that's been forgotten. Parents need to know.
>
> [Many speak at once. "I want specifics!"; "Specifics, yeah!"]
>
> [Norma looks at the group of parents who went to the district school board president and asks them if they want her to speak. Some nod yes.]
>
> Norma: We went to the school board because it seemed to me that it was not going to be possible for our board to resolve this issue. That [there] were a significant amount of people [who] were going to be extremely upset no matter which way the board ruled and as hard as it tried, the board was never going to be able to find that the first grade teacher acted inappropriately, given the

amount of power she has on—with the board.

[A child squeals from the other room. A mother runs out.]

Norma: While I agree that—some people have said to me that they felt this really disrupted our process. I certainly agonized over this before going to the board—

Parent X: [Interrupts] I just want to know if the four people who went to the school board represented the school or themselves.

Chorus: Ourselves—us—our children. And that was made very clear.

Karla: I've tried to stay out of this in a big way. After the parents spoke with [the school board president] he called to speak with me. I told him that the parents are trying to work out a governance system at the school and figure out how to distribute power in the school. He said he didn't care about that. He said "all I want to know is if children are being mistreated and have you observed this." And until a couple of weeks ago I would have said no.

[Complete silence for approximately 5 seconds. Then general talking starts. A kindergarten parent asks Yvonne to give her opinion. Yvonne starts to speak and then begins to cry. A chorus of parents then asked if a board member would address the crowd. The person who steps forward is the outside community member, whom most parents do not know (C*1). He is a family friend and professional colleague of Sara's. Other board members are identified as C* 2, 3, etc.]

C* 1: I'm a member of the board.... Some of you may or may not know me.... [I] don't have a child here at school but I have been heavily involved in education for the last thirty years because I've had two kids that grew up through school.... Over the last two or three months I have been very, very concerned because I've seen the downhill here and what's happening is impacting your children and I'm really really concerned about that.... We're gonna have to determine how we're gonna have a win-win situation. What is it that we need to do to make things happen to make it, make it positive. What is it that we want? ... Now I've been to a couple of meetings and I see the anger and I know that the anger ...

[Board Member C* 1 continues talking around the issue for approximately another five minutes, ending with:]

C* 1: You're at that crossroad tonight....What is it you want? What are your priorities? How are we gonna make it happen? How are we gonna build that trust? If we don't do it tonight I think we're, we're gonna be hurting our kids. So I urge you to really move forward tonight ... step back, count to ten and let's work out a process to make it happen and the board is willing to work with you toward that end.

[Silence. Some parents are looking down, some looking at each other, some whispering. Generally rustling, shifting around. Another board member comes forward to speak to the group. Member B is known among the parents not to be a supporter of Sara. Her daughter is in Sara's classroom.]

C* 2: I've talked to a lot of parents in groups. The problem I have is—there's a few parents I feel who are very vocal ... I appreciate them, but ... [I want to address the fact that many of us parents] are not allowed to really have some power. We're not given ownership of our school. There are a few people who make a lot of the decisions for the school and it—it's not shared and it's not—we—we haven't been brought together to build this as a group.... A lot of parents are frustrated. Parents have told me they won't be back next year and that's what we have to look at as we keep talking about ... We have to understand parents are not wanting to come back next year ... [As she sits down, there is a spattering of applause.]

Parent X: That did not seem like a very board-related comment.

["Yeah, yeah, that's right" from some parents in the crowd. There is general cross talk. Some arguing. Christina, one of the parents who went to the district school board president, asks to speak.]

Christina: I went to speak to [the district school board president] because I wanted to talk about the direction of the school in terms of what happens if Sara, who had threatened to resign, ended up resigning. What happens if she is asked to leave? Will the school board recognize us as an entity? Will they support the charter school? Can we continue the vision? That's what I sat down to talk to [the school board member] about and that's what we started to talk about.

[Clarifications about incidents. Parents ask about details. "Details!" is yelled out from the back. It is now one hour into the meeting.]

Parent L: It says here the board is going to update us on what exactly went down [about Sara being placed on administrative leave] and we haven't heard anything. Your talk was nice [looking at C* 1, the community representative from the board, who had addressed the meeting earlier], but I want the details of what went down.

The overwhelming majority of parents at this meeting—including Sara's opponents—were not in agreement with the four parents who went to the district school board president and felt betrayed by these individuals. The school was in an uproar. The board firmly backed Sara and delivered a statement to the press:

> Conflicts occur and we were mediating it when two parents decided to bring an incident forward. We found nothing abusive, nothing that could be considered out of line.

By the end of April, the district completed its investigation of Sara, and she was cleared of all allegations. Unfortunately, by this time, C-Star's enrollment had dropped from 46 children to 38, and more families were indicating that they would not be returning the following year. Because of the drop in enrollment, the school year faced a dire financial situation. Based on the attendance figures on record through April, ADA funds for the remainder of the school year were less than $8,000, plus the $4,000 in C-Star's discretionary account. The school lacked the necessary revenue to meet operating expenses for the months of May and June. Because energies were so focused on the parent-staff conflict at C-Star, insufficient attention was paid to fund-raising and accountability.[23] Although Sara still had a number of supporters in the school, the membership agreed that she was "a great source of strife and conflict among parents." Therefore, with the majority of the parents' approval, the C-Star Board of Directors voted to "lay Sara off from her position at the school."

Managing Disagreement

Among the most disgruntled C-Star members were Norma and Karla, both of whom were antagonistic to the *social structure* of the organization and began the school year harboring serious misgivings about Sara.[24] Both of these individuals were well educated, vocal, and charismatic, with leadership skills acquired through self-employment and/or serving on nonprofit boards. Over the course of the school year, these two members played significant roles in the turmoil, challenging Sara's decisions and her position of authority in the organization.

It's possible that Norma's and Karla's negative feelings about Sara would have dissolved and carried no weight with the membership if the implementation of the educational program had proceeded without difficulty. In empirical studies on hindsight bias, behavioral science researchers have found that "outcome information consistently influenced evaluations of the quality of a decision, the competence of the decision maker, and the willingness to let the decision maker make decisions for the subject."[25] The disjunction between the C-Star educational program envisioned and the classroom practices witnessed after opening was unsettling for a number of the parents. As they tried to make their concerns known, they perceived barriers, and disgruntled members such as Norma and Karla gained support for their positions regarding Sara and their desire to change the organizational structure. As more and more members perceived that they were not being heard, discord and division escalated, and external concerns such as fund-raising and school district accountability deadlines were tabled.[26]

According to Ann Swidler, if sufficient mechanisms are not available before a school is in operation "for bringing disagreements out into the open, for forging consensus, and for enforcing the collective mandate" (92), a group can find itself lacking the energy to tackle the external pressures that could seriously impact the longevity of the organization. Although unstructured criticism and complaining can be detrimental to a group such as C-Star, carefully designed forums for hearing grievances and evaluating the performance of leaders can maintain the health of an organization. Policies that are in place before operations begin can assure members that their leaders will be held accountable to the group and can assist in educating members about how to participate in governing themselves.[27]

Another dilemma arises, however, in the quest to teach and learn how to constructively disagree in a participatory group. The problem is that the amount of time members must devote to the organization in order to foster this learning infringes on families' and educators' home and work lives. This time factor affects the number and cross-section of parents who can or will involve themselves at this level. A barrier to maintaining internal democracy in an organization such as C-Star is not merely membership apathy, but also the varying daily demands that poor and middle-class families juggle. It is true that uninvolved parents are often more than willing to leave the running of the organization to a small, active minority in exchange for their freedom from meetings and volunteer activities; however, it appears risky for the designated leader(s) of parent or community-based charters to assume that the reason for the membership's uninvolvement is merely apathy.

Second Year of Operations

With the school board's reluctant support, C-Star weathered the financial crisis at the end of the first year by borrowing funds from the district to continue operations. The two teachers, Karla and Yvonne, and approximately half of the first-year families chose not to return for the second year. Although the negative publicity resulting from the first-year turmoil made the recruitment of new families and teachers difficult, the 1995–96 school year opened with 49 children enrolled in two classrooms, a kindergarten and a first/second grade combination.

Among the returning families were three of the original families from Sara's first recruitment effort. Evelyn—founding parent, full-time volunteer, and member of the C-Star board of directors during the first year of operations—assumed informal leadership of C-Star's administrative affairs. She continued to share a seat on the board with her husband (Japanese American), who served as board treasurer and the school's bookkeeper/accountant. Another founding parent (James, European American) who served as the classroom substitute for Sara after she was placed on administrative leave, returned as the first/second grade teacher. Due to the financial situation, the parents did not hire a director and chose to govern the organization with the board of directors, which consisted of five returning parents and three new parents. Norma was elected board president. These returning parents comprised the small working group that labored over the summer months to save the charter school.

Circumstances Change

The desperate need for new families and teachers, in combination with the location of the school being far from the founding families' homes, caused a completely different school culture to evolve in the second year. First of all, the low-income European American families and families of color that C-Star lost from the first year of operations were replaced in the second year by a majority of middle-income, European American families living in or adjacent to the immediate residential neighborhood. In contrast to the ethnic diversity of the first-year board (two African Americans, one Japanese American, and four European Americans), the new board was composed of all European American parents except for the treasurer (Japanese American).

Without the funding for a bus to transport children from the inner city or an aggressive outreach campaign as in the first year, enrollment was totally dependent on those families in the charter school's immediate neighborhood or those who could personally transport their youngsters. This evolution in school demographics marked a significant shift from Sara's original vision of "prioritizing the inclusion of low-income and ethnic minority students" in the enrollment.

The second factor impacting the school culture was the difference in second-year parents' motivations for enrolling their children in C-Star. A large number of the new parents entering the school did not enroll their children because of an attraction to the C-Star educational program or because of the unique role of parents in the school. According to Lorraine, who returned the second year to serve as a volunteer education consultant,

> A lot of these [new] parents are at [C-Star] by default because they couldn't get in their school of choice. They're just marking time until they do.... They're not committed to the charter school.

Other parents chose C-Star because it was a small school and/or because it was located in or near their neighborhood.

In the scramble to save the school, the C-Star recruitment committee abandoned the process of carefully orienting new families to the mission and concentrated on boosting the enrollment in order to stay open. As a result, the organization gained a large number of parents who did not volunteer or attend meetings; nor did they respond to communications from the Board or inquiries that dealt with general school issues. For most of these parents, the only two-way school communication was with their child's teacher, concerning issues that related directly to the student.

As far as the second-year teaching staff, the Board did not have a large pool of applicants from which to choose at the beginning of the year. The result was a staff (two Caucasians, one Latina) with little knowledge or working experience in the educational philosophies and strategies that formed the basis for the existing program. The teacher with the most knowledge of Sara's original educational vision was James; however, he too was struggling in the second year to merge his practice with the theories underlying the program. Because of the inexperience of the teachers, the board drew up one-year contracts stipulating that evaluations would be held later in the year to determine if the teachers would continue in their positions the following year.

Without an experienced educational coordinator or head teacher on staff to chart a course for professional development, the individual teachers were pretty much on their own. The pedagogy and curriculum in one classroom appeared to be based on a traditional, teacher-centered model; and the other appeared more child-centered and developmental.

A Research and Development working group was formed to assist the teachers with adapting their classroom practices to the C-Star educational philosophy. Lorraine, who was serving on this committee, found it frustrating because of the lack of commitment on the part of the teachers:

> I was really invested in doing this at first but now I wonder if what I'm invested in is possible.... I don't know if people [teachers] want to spend the time to get Reggio—take the time to pull together the philosophy and merge it with actual practice. There aren't enough people who believe in the integrity of the practice.... In one meeting they said "we can't do Reggio" because they don't have the resources ... and there's so much pressure to do projects, but when I went into the classroom and kids were working on [a project], they couldn't articulate what it was they were doing or why. The art teacher told me what they were doing, but the kids couldn't talk about it.... The individual agendas—the parents' individual agendas.... Like [James], for instance, he said that he's teaching Spanish because of [Norma]. But then I think, if he had a stronger curriculum, people wouldn't be after him to do something else.

Board members were aware of and concerned about the lack of coherence in the educational program but were primarily focused on paying off the debt to the school board and keeping the school fiscally afloat during the first semester. In an interview, Norma questioned their process:

> We're still trying to deal with the ed program that was set up by Sara... Why are we doing this? We've lost a lot of kids because people are not excited about what is going on in the classroom.... [And besides] we may not be in a position to pay back our debt to the district like we said we would.

By December, C-Star's enrollment had dropped from 49 students to 37, with exiting parents citing their dissatisfaction with "what's going on in the classroom" as the reason for disenrolling their children. Parents who had no other alternative but C-Star appealed directly to their children's individual teachers to make changes to the classroom curriculum. Only a minority of parents, primarily returning parents, took their concerns to the board.

Teacher Evaluations

Toward the beginning of the second semester, the C-Star Board turned its attention fully to the teacher evaluation process that would determine whether the teachers' contracts would be renewed the following year. An educational consultant, recommended by the school district, was hired to assist the board in designing a procedure for the evaluation. A series of strategic planning meetings were also scheduled on Saturdays to address revisions to the mission, the vision, and the educational program.

In parent meetings and newsletters, the board asked for participation and input from the general membership in the evaluation process. At the same time, surveys were mailed home to solicit parent opinions about C-Star's overall education program. The surveys did not contain questions concerning teacher performance, but rather focused on the curriculum content. Approximately 50% of the parents completed and returned their surveys, but no parents came forth to participate in the evaluation process.

As a result of the teacher observations conducted by the outside educational consultant and board members, plus self-assessments completed by the individual teachers, all of the teachers were informed in April that their contracts would not be renewed for the following year. They were invited by the board to reapply for their present positions, with the explanation that their applications would be placed in a pool along with those of new candidates. Although the teachers had been aware that this was a possibility, the actual decision was upsetting to them. Speaking for the staff at a board meeting following the announcement, James argued that they had faced intolerable difficulties:

> I think the commitment that teachers have had to meet is over the top! Meetings, time, no money for materials.... This is not like the public schools. We didn't have benefits until December. There was tremendous insecurity.... Staff meetings were dominated by program development.... The amount of stress.... I feel we were asked to do a lot, and now being asked to reapply?

Although they followed the evaluation process and recommendations suggested by their educational consultant, the board members were also torn about the final decision. C-Star's educational program was based on teachers collaborating and creating a cohesive schoolwide curriculum. The board members liked the teachers as individuals but agreed that they did not collaborate well because of their disparate philosophies. However, individual board members differed in their opinions about the fairness of the evaluation process. Some believed that the process was too closed and that parents and teachers should have played a more central role in working out a solution. Other board members felt strongly that they had provided plenty of opportunities for the parents to participate and that it was their job, as the board of directors, to evaluate the teachers and decide "what was best for the school as a whole."

The following excerpts are from a three-page memo about the teacher evaluations that was sent to the parent community from the C-Star board:

> As we explained at the last parent meeting, we did not wish to directly tie a teacher's contract decision to the just-completed evaluation. We felt that it would be better to give detailed goals and objectives during the evaluation and allow each teacher some time to implement the recommendations before making this decision, even if it meant waiting until later to make final staffing decisions. On the other hand, our teachers were not unknown quantities to us. We had several months of observing how they worked in their individual classrooms, in the school generally and with each other, and had been

> through one evaluation process with them eight weeks after school started.
>
> As a very new organization, and particularly in light of the difficult first year we had, we felt a strong responsibility to the school to ensure that we had the best teachers possible on staff. We also were taking into consideration the large number of parents who, literally, voted with their feet earlier in the year. Many parents who left the school, while supportive of the descriptions contained in our charter, voiced concerns about what they saw as a lack of clear direction and educational mission. No school can survive for long with the 20% attrition each year.

After giving the reasons for conducting the evaluation, the memo detailed the process:

> In January, [the consultant] began to work with the Board of Directors, staff and interested community members on long-term planning and curriculum development. As part of this, staff members drafted new program and job descriptions with [the consultant]. Using these documents, [the consultant] developed the observation and teacher assessment tools she and the Board members used for the evaluation. In preparation, each teacher was given a Self-Assessment form to complete, which asked the individual teachers to assess their own strengths and weaknesses in each of the areas addressed (see the copies of each available in the school office). [The consultant's] contract also included several hours of observation time in each classroom, a detailed written report of what she observed, and descriptions of the matches and variances from our program description. She offered each teacher the opportunity to receive feedback on his or her individual classroom at the end of these observations.

The kindergarten teacher appealed directly to her students' parents, who rallied to her defense to challenge the board's decision. Other parents were quickly drawn into the dispute and mounted a united front to lobby for all three teachers. For the first time during the year, parents turned out in droves for school meetings to debate the decision. For many parents, this issue sparked their first glimmer of interest in the fact that C-Star was a charter school and that board elections were slated for the next month. The following excerpt is from one of the parent meetings where the evaluation decision was being discussed. Thirty-five people were in attendance, and the spokesperson for the board is Harriet, a returning parent from the first year of operations. (C* 3 indicates a C-Star Board Member other than Harriet.)

Harriet: I want to give some history on how the decision was reached.... Our responsibility as a board is to the whole school, not just our own kids. We had a very difficult time making the decision to open up the hiring process. None of the board are professionals in this area so ... it was really hard...

Parent A: When will the teachers know if they're going to be hired back?

Harriet: They will know as soon as ... as early in May as possible.

Parent B: Did they get poor evaluations?

Harriet: Staff evaluations are confidential so—

Parent B: [Interrupting] Can the staff say it's okay for us to know?

Harriet: There are legal—are legal issues involved with this... We have to say that the staff is the very best the we can get. You may look at this in a few weeks and have the same staff.... It's really not an unusual situation—

Parent C: [Interrupting] Since this is a new school—we're just developing and we don't have structures.... We don't have an evaluation process that is fair and consistent. Parents should be involved in this. Evaluations should.... They should be ongoing, shouldn't they?

Harriet: We did do an evaluation after eight weeks into the school year and the second one is now...

Parent D: One thing that sold me on this school was the interactions I saw going on with the staff and students.... It upsets me that this may not be the case.

Parent F: Is the board decision final?

[Cross talk.]

Parent G: I'm the kindergarten representative, and there have never been negative comments that I know of about the kindergarten teacher. I like the kindergarten teacher and I think my daughter would be very distraught to know that you're...

C* 3: As a board member, in no way was this decision a vote of no confidence ... We want to hear your opinions. Please express yourselves.

Parent G: Well, what is it then if it wasn't a vote of no confidence? What are you saying? I don't understand.

Parent D: You can't do this to teachers, can you? I thought, I thought—Why aren't we going by the public school union rules?

Harriet: Because we are a charter school.

Parent Z: What does that mean?

Harriet: You need to read the charter and the bylaws... They're on file in the office.

Parent C: I haven't read the charter but I know this is not the point to hire new teachers.

Harriet: In the bylaws these decisions are under the jurisdiction of the board, but you may recall the board.

Parent C: If enough parents disagree you can recall the board?

[Parents turn to one another and begin gesturing and talking. The board members look at each other.]

As the parents proceeded to ask more questions about how to reverse the decision (e.g., changing the bylaws; recalling board members, nominating and electing new parents in the upcoming election, etc.), the board members began to express their frustration about trying to govern the school without the participation of the majority of parents in the school. Two complaints by board members recorded from this general meeting summarize the board's response to the C-Star parents:

> We have open board meetings. We're parents, too. We're not some separate big, bad group.
>
> When you don't contribute and then you complain, it makes me mad.

Although the board members appealed to the parents in the general meeting that they were "parents, too" and not some separate group, the *role-demands* and their *role-performance* as "The Board" contributed to their own personal feelings that they were a separate group that operated apart from the majority of C-Star parents. Consider some of the responsibilities of the board:

- Paying off the school's debt to the district while maintaining operations on a limited budget;
- Lobbying the school board to improve C-Star's image;
- Leading the restructuring of the school's curriculum and pedagogy;
- Maintaining enrollment numbers to prevent a decrease in the ADA; and
- Recruiting new families to the school.

Board members labored many evening and weekend hours over the course of the year to meet these demands, without support or assistance from a majority of the C-Star parents. Because of the low attendance at board meetings, general parent meetings, and planning workshops, as well as the minimal home-to-school communication, it was difficult for board members not to view themselves or behave as leaders/managers in a *service organization*—making decisions for clients who did not know or care about what would best serve their own interests.

Months before the evaluation incident, there was an awareness among board members—via rumors and innuendoes—that they were considered by the general parent body to be "wielding too much power." At a long-range planning meeting in January at which three teachers and all board members were in attendance, the issue of power was discussed:

Norma: I feel uncomfortable with all the gossip and innuendos flying around about people wielding too much power and people having hidden agendas. This needs to be brought out directly.... I don't think it's helpful so let's put it on the table—this issue of power—let's just put it on the table.

Evelyn: Do you mean—Do you mean the board? Where is this coming from? Are you talking about the board?

C* 3: No, the rest of the parents. They don't come to meetings and they don't read anything. If they don't come, the only thing we can do is inform them.

Harriet: I think it's just the nature of the —It's just—I think everyone is just interested in educating their kids and it's an emotional thing—an emotional issue ... so—

Evelyn: I'm glad people have power. We wouldn't get anything done if someone didn't exercise power.

C* 4: I agree with [Evelyn and Harriet]. We're developing something unique here, and that means uncomfortableness, and we're going to disagree.... Someone has to take charge and whoever does that is going to be in the hot seat.

Harriet: Yes, and we as board members have to make difficult decisions that—that someone is—is always going to complain about, but that doesn't mean we have to jump whenever someone complains.

Art teacher: Trust takes time.... What we're doing is new and we don't know each other that well. We

> don't know if we can trust each other, so we have to be courageous.

Those board members who had been around for the first year of operations, especially Norma, found it particularly ironic to be fielding complaints that were reminiscent of their own first-year criticisms of Sara. Norma did not feel, however, that the board "had any choice but to keep moving forward."

The minimal involvement that characterized the majority of the parents' participation up to the time of teacher evaluations obscured from board members the possibility that the disparate group of parents would unite and oppose the board decision. It appears that the board did not factor in the weight of the relationships that had developed over the year between the teachers and their students' parents. Even though the C-Star parents were lukewarm about curriculum and pedagogy, personal loyalties had formed over the course of the year between the parents and their children's individual teachers. In contrast, no personal bonds or collegial connections had been fostered between the new parents and the board.

As a result of the contract turmoil, those board members who were not fully in accord with the evaluation process rescinded their support and agreed to revisit the decision after the soon-to-be-held election for the 1996–97 board of directors. The two board members who were the most committed to the nonrenewal of the teachers' contracts—a father who had disenrolled his child from C-Star earlier in the year and Norma, the board president—chose not to run for office for the next term. All other incumbents were reelected to the board for the following year, along with two new parents. One of the first decisions made by the new board was to renew the teachers' contracts for the next school year.

Over half of the families and one teacher chose not return to C-Star for the 1996–97 school year. Regardless of the large turnover and shakiness of the educational program after the second year, a host of new families, predominantly European American, replaced those who left and C-Star expanded, adding a 3/4 classroom to the program. An educational coordinator was hired to oversee teacher development and evaluation.

In the third year of operations the school continued to struggle, but Evelyn reported in the second semester that the school appeared to be slowly gaining some sense of stability:

> We had a horrible fall. We hired someone for the second grade and then they left after the first few days of school—She was making a career change .... had been teaching preschool and this was just too different. [She] hated—just found it awful to be under the microscope all the time ... James and [the kindergarten teacher] are still here.... Every class has a waiting list of students and our relationship with the school district is really good. I think we really gained credibility and some respect when we paid off that [debt]. Oh ... who had a big hand in getting us respect was Harriet. Savvy. [She was] politically savvy.... I now have a contact and I know how to deal with them [the district]. I can (laughing) shuffle all the right papers. I learned by the seat of my pants what to do—

Organizational Evolution

The organizational model initially proposed for C-Star by Sara and idealized by the first-year parents closely mirrors that of the *mutual-benefit association*. The prime beneficiary is the membership—the charter school families, with parents and guardians responsible for meeting the structural requirements of maintaining the organization. The parents strongly embraced this model and believed that this was the organizational and governing structure of their school, even though they approved bylaws that contradicted it. As mentioned earlier in the chapter, one of the crucial issues facing a *mutual-benefit association* is internal democracy. Considering typical parent involvement patterns, this type of organizational structure seems particularly problematic for parent-driven charter enterprises. Due to lack of time, daily work and home pressures, and/or minimal knowledge in the management of organizations, there is a tendency for the majority of parents to willingly turn over control and leadership to an active minority.

In both the first and second years, those individuals who assumed responsibility for the school's operations had to become knowledgeable about the intricacies and dilemmas the organization was facing. The experience of the parents serving on the second-year board reveals the role this knowledge played in affecting how they governed and their relationships with staff and other parents. As their understanding of charter funding and accountability (e.g., the relationships of enrollment to financial stability, accountability to educational program) developed, the parents on the board grew more conscious of the market-driven concerns—efficiency, survival, competition—of the organization. Their initial decision not to renew the teachers' contracts was influenced in part by the belief that the teachers' performances were a liability to the marketability of the school. Although the C-Star board of parents eventually yielded to the larger group and reversed their decision, the fact that a primary reason for non-renewal of teacher contracts was to maintain and/or increase enrollment is key to the charter concept. In contrast, the traditional public school can operate for decades with marginal curriculum and teacher performance without a hint of closing. Charter school operators cannot lose sight of the fact that they are also a *business concern* that needs to attract clients and remain competitive in the "school market."

The critical intersection in charter schools of enrollment, educational program, and funding became visible to those serving in leadership positions in C-Star while remaining largely invisible to the majority of the parent body. This made it difficult—even for those members who argued strongly for the *mutual-benefit* model in the first year—not to adopt the attitude of *service organization* decision-makers ruling for clients who were ignorant of the big picture.

In addition, charter operators cannot restrict their focus to the bottom line or to the pleasing of their particular constituency. Although decentralized and deregulated in varying degrees, charter schools are public schools that are supposed to be held accountable by an external sponsor for student achievement, financial management, health and safety, and equity in enrollment. Although charters have been and are being questioned and challenged on their perceived violations in these areas, the courts have so far upheld the public status of these schools. Charter schools are *commonweal organizations* responsible for the socialization and training of the young for their future roles in society.

Therefore, "Who owns the charter school?" Charter school parents, students, and staff, as well as the public at large, are all stakeholders in this enterprise if we follow Sarason's political principle:

> [W]hen you are going to be affected, directly or indirectly, by a decision, you should stand in some relationship to the decision-making process. [28]

So is it in the best interest of all the stakeholders for parents to adopt a *mutual-benefit association* model for the organizational structure of the charter school?

For C-Star, the time and energy expended to maintain enrollment, financial solvency, and internal democracy diminished the organization's ability to effectively implement the educational goals of the founding mission and safeguard the objectives of the public at large. Would more preparation and planning time before operations have eased some of the beginning chaos? Or would a more cohesive and involved founding group of parents have been able to avoid some of the pitfalls that C-Star encountered?

The focus of the next case study is Community Charter School, which opened its doors two years after C-Star in a nearby county. The parents of Community Charter knew about C-Star's first-year turmoil and used the information to avoid some of the same mistakes. More time and attention went into developing operating systems and procedures before opening and the founders made the conscious decision to chart the beginning course by themselves, without the leadership of a professional educator.

NOTES

1. Key to symbols used in quotations:
   Three dots (...) indicate omission of words within a sentence.
   Four dots (....) indicate omission of complete sentence(s).
   Dashes (—) between words indicate connections or clarifications of trains of thought.
   Dashes (—) at the end of a block of text indicate respondent's intention of continuing to speak.

2. Carolyn Edwards, Leila Gandini, and George Forman, *The Hundred Languages of Children* (Norwood, NJ: Ablex Publishing Corporation, 1993).

3. The accompanying footnote in the charter petition explains that C-Star's approach to mathematics was derived from *The Nuffield Math Materials* by John Wiley & Company (1967). The approach employs hands-on experience and representation of experience through charts, drawings, and graphs.

4. The charter petition cites the 1974 Vancouver Project, headed by Selma Wassermann at Simon Fraser University. Wassermann found that children using the Ashton-Warner approach were reading at the same level as the traditional reading program, even though all of the children were assessed with tests formulated for the traditional reading program. Additionally, the Ashton-Warner students scored substantially higher in their attitudes toward reading than those children learning from traditional programs.

5. Yancey, "Parents as Partners."

6. Ann Swidler, *Organization without Authority* (Cambridge: Harvard University Press, 1979).

7. Emil Durkheim, *The Division of Labor in Society*, trans. G. Simpson (New York: Free Press, 1964. Originally published in 1893).

8. Ibid.; Emil Durkheim, *Suicide: A Study in Sociology*, trans. J. A. Spalding and G. Simpson (New York: Free Press, 1951. Originally published in 1897).

9. Sara's and Karla's stories about Sara's recruitment/hiring process mirror one of the pitfalls that Blau & Scott emphasize about *mutual-benefit associations:* "The very enthusiasm that marks the activities of the devoted original members leads them to attempt to persuade others of the moral superiority of their beliefs, and such proselytizing brings in new members less strongly identified with the goals of the association." Blau and Scott, *Formal Organizations*, 46.

10. M. D. Cohen, J. G. March, and P. J. Olsen, "A Garbage-Can Model of Organizational Choice," *Administrative Science Quarterly* 17.1 (1972), cited in Butler, "Time in Organizations," 935–37. Decision making in a *garbage-can organization*—"an organization in which there is high ambiguity about technology, problems, solutions, and participants"—can be haphazard and occur in a *spasmodic* way. "Individual decision issues may not be able to receive all the time that decision-makers might like to give to them since other issues coming up for consideration can crowd out an existing issue."

11. *Social structure.* In utilizing this term, Newton and Levinson emphasize two components of structure: the division of labor and the division of authority. In more formal organizations, positions are formally defined and permanent; they are typically changed through a redefinition of organizational structure, not through the comings and goings of individuals. Individuals in formally structured working groups occupy positions and take roles. *Role-performance* is structurally based in requirements that accompany a given position. However, even in formal working groups, requirements are usually ambiguous enough to allow the individual *role-performance* to be shaped also by the personality, background experience, and such, of the individual worker. The more roles and tasks there are, the more need there is for

activities to be integrated and coordinated. In order to do this, someone must have the responsibility for the ordering and coordination. "Responsibility requires that one have the authority—the legitimate right—to make demands, exert influence, and impose sanctions. Organizations are stratified in order to achieve the integration necessary to the fulfillment of complex tasks." Peter M. Newton and Daniel J. Levinson, "The Work Group within the Organization: A Sociopsychological Approach," *Psychiatry* 36 (1973): 115–42, 126.

12. One married couple shared a single board seat.

13. A. Nicholls, *Managing Educational Innovations* (London: George Allen & Unwin, 1983), 75.

14. Joe Nathan, from the Center for School Change at the University of Minnesota, argues that it is imperative that charter school teachers and administrators inform parents, consistently and thoroughly, about what the school is doing and what their kids are learning. He warns: "If [parents] do not understand, they will question, complain and make bigtime trouble. This is their right. You can head this off by helping parents understand what your notion of learning is and by constantly sharing what's going on." Joe Nathan, *Charter Schools: Creating Hope and Opportunity for American Education* (San Francisco: Jossey-Bass Publishers, 1996), 5, 6.

15. Joyce A. Rothschild-White, "Conditions Facilitating Participatory-Democratic Organizations," *Sociological Inquiry* 46 (1976): 70–86.

16. Swidler, *Organization without Authority,* 83.

17. Ibid., 1.

18. Butler, "Time in Organizations," 935. See note 10 above. In *spasmodic time,* the present is experienced "through events

that are irregular, highly novel, movable, and with many concurrent events also impinging."

19. On the issue of governance in schools, Sarason explains that for many individuals, the critical importance of governance is hard to grasp because "it does not denote a thing, but rather the allocation, distribution, and uses of power to achieve stated goals for an entity." Parents may understand their relationships with others in terms of "local rules and goals of governance, but very few understand how those relationships are determined by rules and goals of the larger structure." Sarason, *Parental Involvement*, 1.

20. In "The Work Group within the Organization: A Sociopsychological Approach," Newton and Levinson define *social process* as "How a group works... from the highly rational forms of planning, problem solving, and collaborative use of technical skills to the most irrational forms of destruction of any real work as well as exploitation and humiliation of members"(117). Recurring themes are important. Widely shared feelings and fantasies about collective life, as well as what the group actually does, create the *social process*. "Often, group members are so submerged in the process that dominant themes go unnoticed" (134).

21. In "Roles, Personality, and Social Structure in the Organizational Setting," Levinson explains that the individual effects his/her modes of adaptation while operating within a "complex system of requirements, facilities, and conditions of work"(175). There are two levels of adaptation: the ideational (*role-conception*) and the behavioral (*role-performance*). *Role-conception* is formed partially within the given organization, but is also influenced by an individual's "childhood experiences, by his (her) values and other personality characteristics, by formal education and apprenticeship and the like" (176). *Role-performance* is also the result of a number of forces. Some of these forces are external, such as the *role-demands* of a particular position and pressure from one's superiors in an organization. Informal group influ-

ences and impending sanctions can also impact *role-performance*. Other determinants are internal, such as one's *role-conceptions* and personality traits that are relevant to the particular role.

22. Ibid.

23. Yancey, "Parents as Partners."

24. Newton and Levinson, "The Work Group."

25. J. Baron and J. C. Hershey, "Outcome Bias in Decision Evaluation," *Journal of Personality and Social Psychology* 34 (1988): 240–47, cited by Scott A. Hawkins and Reid Hastie in "Hindsight: Judgments of Past Events after the Outcomes are Known," *Psychological Review* 107 (1990): 311–27, 320.

26. Swidler, *Organization without Authority.*

27. Ibid.; Joyce A. Rothschild-White, "Conditions."

28. Sarason, *Parental Involvement*, 7.

CHAPTER FOUR

SEARCHING FOR DIVERSITY

In the spring of 1994, a parent meeting was held at an urban, middle-income preschool in California to discuss the Reggio Emilia early childhood education philosophy. The guest speaker for the session was Sara, the founder and first-year director of C-Star. Over the course of the evening, the primary focus of the group discussion shifted to the topic of charter schools. As a result of the positive interest generated from parents at that meeting, two of the mothers actively began to recruit a small group to research the feasibility of founding an elementary charter school in their community. Initial recruitment was via word of mouth. One father's description of how he became involved was similar to the stories recalled by his colleagues:

> [One of the couples] lived across the street and we were talking about the preschool that their kid went to and the preschool my kid went to, and they were telling me about this thing they were involved in. And I said I would maybe be interested in coming to a meeting—[1]

As a result of this informal beginning and outreach process, seven parents (two fathers and five mothers; a total of six families) of preschool to elementary-age children joined together to form Community Charter's founding core group. All of the parents—six European Americans and one Latina—were well-educated professionals, from middle- to upper-income family backgrounds, and politically self-identified as liberal/progressive. At the time of the initial organizing drive, all had children who were of preschool or elementary school age. One founding member was a health coordinator at a local Head Start center, one mother was a lesbian midwife, and the two fathers worked at the community law center that represented primarily low-income families. George, one of the fathers whose leadership role was pivotal to the petitioning campaign and the opening of the charter school, described himself during an interview as having been involved "for the last ten years in radical, political work."

In the initial planning meetings, the founders decided on four foundational elements for their school's educational vision:

- An antibias, developmentally appropriate curriculum;
- Governance and decision making shared by students, parents, and teachers;
- Small class sizes;
- The promotion and fostering of diversity—socioeconomic, racial, cultural, family structure, and sexual orientation—throughout the organization.

Although all four principles—antibias curriculum, student-parent-teacher run, small classes, and diversity—were integral parts of the vision, diversity appeared to be the most central component. It informed Community Charter's curriculum, hiring, and governance policies, as well as decisions on classroom practices and after-school services.

The following excerpts from comments by four of the founders reveal the personal and political backgrounds and motivations that shaped this vision—the *ethos and values*—of Community Charter:[2]

> Because I'm a parent, it's the main motivation ... my kids are at that age. My son is already attending public school. His class has 26 kids. I feel there's lots that public schools can do, but they're not willing to do it.

> I grew up in Louisiana [and] where you had your kids [enrolled in school] was as about as political a statement you could make in the '60s and '70s.... I grew up in a household where my parents were very adamant about having their kids in public schools and in working in the public schools. [The public schools] were forcibly integrated right around the time I was starting and a lot of people took their kids out so I have very strong feelings about their importance.

> Conventional, chronological progression, that advances kids grade by grade in the public school system regardless if they're achieving or not, is wrong ... a lot of children—and not just poor or minority kids—are falling through the cracks because their individual needs are not being addressed.

> [T]o actively utilize an anti-bias curriculum to confront the "isms" that are so pervasive in our society—racism, heterosexualism, sexism ... this is the kind of education I want for my child.

The founding group believed strongly that their educational vision contrasted radically to that of the Manzanita district public schools. During their petitioning process, they passionately argued that there were "deep philosophical differences" between the Community Charter vision and the school district's approach to education. The local school board and teachers' union president were unconvinced and claimed that there was nothing these parents "want that can't be or isn't already being done in existing [Manzanita] schools." Nevertheless, the parents maintained that it was their dissatisfaction with the system, and the public school choices that were available to them, that motivated them to organize.[3]

Ethos and Values vs. Organizational Timeline

As mentioned, of the four cornerstones in the Community Charter educational vision, diversity appeared to be the core component. This perception about its central importance in the mission was not shared by all founders, however. For some of the founders, diversity was the nucleus of the vision; for others, diversity was just one of four equally important components. These different beliefs about its role/importance in the mission and the difficulties the founding group experienced in actually diversifying its membership became the most problematic of the implementation challenges that faced Community Charter.

Because of the lack of racial and socioeconomic diversity of the founding members themselves, problems were experienced as soon as the group launched its public campaign. The 1992 California charter law encourages sponsors to give preferential consideration to petitions that target academically at-risk students.[4] While the state law does not require charter schools to serve only underserved populations, local school boards have the option of using this factor in deciding whether or not to support a petition. A local newspaper described the Community Charter parent group—after their first appearance before the school board, approximately five months after their initial organizing meeting—as "majority white or Asian, with one or two African American parents and a few Latinos" and "lawyers and other professionals." Reports such as this did not assist Community Charter parents in making their case for an alternative public school seem urgent, nor did it help their outreach efforts to families of color. A Filipina student teacher who attended a general meeting after learning about the group through friends described her first impression:

> I was curious, always looking for potential jobs you know, so I went to this meeting and walked in and instantly immediately thought to myself, "They're all white!" There were actually a couple of Asians I think, but not enough of.... It turned me off. In [Manzanita]? They were nice people, friendly, but it turned me off and made me kind of suspicious and I wondered how other people feel—How would it feel for a poor Latino family

> or black family? Wouldn't—Would you feel like hanging out?

In plotting their course of action, Community Charter founders wrestled with the dilemma of whether to first concentrate their energies on diversifying the initial founding group, or move ahead with the official petitioning process before the school board and designate recruitment as a secondary task. The issue of time—specifically a lack of it—appeared to be the key factor in their decision to move ahead first with getting their charter petition approved. The sources of the time pressure were both internal and external. Internally, the primary source of pressure came from the parents themselves. As in the C-Star parents' case, the Community Charter parents were organizing because their children were either ready to enter kindergarten or already enrolled in an elementary school that parents wanted to leave. Externally, the time pressure originated from the particulars of the state law. The 1992 California charter legislation limited the number of charter schools (100) that could be approved across the state.[5] For the founders, the possibility of "losing out on getting a number" weighed heavily in their decision making and overrode their concerns about diversifying the founding group. As one founder (Carl) explained:

> We decided in fall 1994 to go for a strategy where we moved very quickly, as quickly as possible, [to get our petition] to the board. There were 65 charter schools that had been approved. We felt, Oh, there are only 35 left, we have to get going! ... We had a draft concept of how we would do broad community outreach that would have started the process of diversifying our group ... but we set that aside and focused on [bringing our petition to] the board.

Although the group scheduled a community meeting every three weeks to recruit new members—in addition to pursuing their primary task of petitioning—it became apparent over time that this was not going to be sufficient to recruit substantial numbers of marginalized families to their charter effort. The majority of families they were attracting by their public flyers and community meetings were European American and from middle-income backgrounds.

Political Opposition

Community Charter was the first charter school in the Manzanita district to petition the local school board for sponsorship. When the parents launched the campaign, the district was in the midst of implementing a system-wide seismic safety program and reconfiguring its grade level groupings to achieve better racial balance in its elementary and middle schools. Board elections were also slated for the same semester, and a new school district superintendent had just been hired. In a December newspaper article, the school board president addressed the charter issue:

> It's good to see parents as excited and involved in education.... But this would be a dramatic change. With all the changes and upheavals in the [Manzanita] schools, a charter school might be difficult to assimilate right now.

Because the Manzanita and neighboring school districts of Community Charter are highly heterogeneous, with racial and socioeconomic diversity at the forefront of educational policymakers' discussions and reform attempts, the founders' lack of diversity translated into a major political barrier to charter approval. Charter foes, from the beginning, have argued that one of the potential dangers of the movement is the reinstitution of segregated schools through the "creaming" of middle-class White families and middle-class families of color from the public schools.[6] The "middle-class group of professionals" petitioning the local school board on behalf of Community Charter appeared to be, as the school board president said, already "well served by the district."

Another potential political barrier, identified early on by other charter school operators in the vicinity, was the local teachers' union. Although Community Charter was advised that union "opposition was likely," the parents were not discouraged by the warnings. As one of the founders explained:

> We didn't think it was going to be a happy relationship, but we [believed] we would figure out a way to work out some relationship.

Heeding the warnings of their colleagues, Community Charter began sending formal letters of introduction to school board members and the local teachers' union president as soon as a solid draft of the charter was available. The following is an excerpt from the introductory letter to the union president:

> As [one of the founders] mentioned to you on the phone yesterday, we are very interested in getting your suggestions for changes and additions to this draft charter. We have intentionally left blank the sections on teacher benefits, etc., awaiting your input. As a group, we are committed to working with and supporting the [Manzanita teachers' union] throughout the planning and operation phases of the public charter school. This not only includes a commitment to compensating all teachers commensurate with current union wages and benefits, but also the possibility of placing a [union] member on the public charter school Board of Directors.
>
> We would like to meet with you as soon as possible to discuss the draft charter and any other issues you may have.

In her response, the union president said that the union would support the charter school if it included a collective bargaining agreement in the charter petition. The founders agreed and added the collective bargaining clause to the final draft, and in October they began their solicitation of the district teacher signatures required for the petition's submission for approval.[7] After the initial response from the president, direct communications from the union ceased. In one letter to a sympathetic school board member, Community Charter expressed its frustration in trying to make contact with the union president:

> We have probably left 10 messages for her on various phone machines, and have not heard back.... After giving an initial indication of openness, [the union president] has completely rebuffed us, refusing even to meet with us.

At school board meetings and in the press, the local teachers' union president emerged as a fierce and vocal opponent of the charter petition. She argued that charters were a threat to collective bargaining and could potentially turn back the clock to pre-union days when teachers were "disrespected, overworked, and underpaid" by the school system. She emphasized strongly in an interview that

> the rights of workers must be considered equally to the rights of parents. There is a danger because we do not have the ability to regulate what happens in those schools... There are many questions to consider such as will there be uncertified parents or persons teaching in the classroom? [This is] unacceptable ... [There are] too many loose regulations with these schools—[8]

Out in the community, the founders "beefed up" their outreach and started holding public meetings every three weeks. The word was spreading, and by December general meetings were attracting up to 25 people. The founders gathered the requisite 10 teacher signatures and formally submitted their petition to the school board in December. Approximately one week after the signatures were filed, Manzanita schools began to receive union flyers outlining reasons for teachers to oppose charter schools in general. Two Manzanita district teachers later recalled that the literature distributed contained information about the threat charter schools posed to the working conditions of teachers and urged them not to sign any charter petitions.

At a school board meeting held one month later, the local union president presented a letter to the board signed by seven of the ten teachers who had originally signed in support of Community Charter's petition. The letter requested the recision of their signatures from the charter petition. The reason cited for the teachers' withdrawal of support was that the teachers were "misled as to the purpose of the petition." The union president explained that the teachers had signed the petition because they believed that they would be considered for jobs at the new school. Prior to the meeting, Community Charter had received no indications that the teachers were concerned or that they wished to withdraw their support. The teachers in question did not attend the board meeting, nor did they respond to inquiries to discuss their actions. One founder recalled:

> We never got the story. I knew one of them actually.... I was the one who got her signature. I left a message on her voice mail. I told her if she doesn't want to talk about it she can leave a message on my voice mail, but please leave a message. She never returned my call. Yeah, it's intense—like in the movies.

The Manzanita school board deferred the decision about whether to accept the recision of the signatures to the district legal counsel and postponed the vote on the petition. In the interim, Community Charter gathered 10 more teacher signatures to replace the rescinded signatures, continued to lobby the union, the community, and the board, and recruited families of 67 children to sign preliminary enrollment forms (37.3% European American, 29.9% African American, 22.4% Asian, 13.4% Latino, 3% Native American). One month after receiving the union letter rescinding the original teachers' signatures, the school board denied Community Charter's petition, citing legal counsel's advice that the rescinded signatures rendered the petition invalid. Several Manzanita board members explained that the lack of support for the charter school was primarily because of the vagueness of the petition and lingering concerns that the charter school would rob funds from other district schools.

After the board decision most of the newly recruited families abandoned the group; however, the initial founders decided to appeal. One founder recalled:

> A lot of people heard about this and thought we were dead. So they went away. There were only five or six of

> us that thought we could navigate the appeal process and come out the other end.... Even with this group it was a struggle to keep positive. I found myself in a lot of debates about whether it was realistic to appeal.... People didn't think much of an appeal except maybe it would be a moral victory.

The 1992 California legislation allowed petitioners to appeal to their county board of education if their charter was denied by the district. The county would then convene a review panel to determine whether the local district board had acted arbitrarily in denying the petition. If the review panel found in favor of the charter group, the petitioners could resubmit their case to the original sponsor.[9] Community Charter appealed their case to the Warren County Office of Education and won. The county review panel determined that the teachers' signatures were in place at the time Community Charter's petition was filed with Manzanita district and should have been accepted. The following is an excerpt from the letter sent to the Manzanita school board president from the county superintendent:

> After reviewing the documentation and hearing the arguments of the appellants and the [Manzanita] representatives during a public hearing, the Review Panel voted four to three in favor of remanding the charter school proposal back to the district governing board for reconsideration.
>
> The Review Panel determined that the teachers' signatures which qualified the petition for consideration were in place on December 7, 1994 when the petition was submitted to the Board and that the petition should have been considered on its merits. Thus, in accordance with Education Code 47605(j)(2), the Review Panel concluded that the district governing board had not appropriately considered the charter school petition.

The victory was sweet for the parents, as one founder recalled with glee:

> You should have seen [the superintendent's] face. He was so angry. I mean they counted us out! They thought we were just a bunch of crazy parents.

The celebratory feelings were brief, however. After repetitioning the Manzanita school board in May, the parents were again denied approval by a vote of 4-1. The school board, on the recommendation of the district superintendent, rejected the petition due to "insufficient detail" in areas such as "payroll, transportation, custodial and food service" and "how racial and ethnic balance would be achieved" in the charter school. The founders believed that they had been treated unfairly because their repeated attempts to contact and discuss the details of their petition with district staff had been ignored. The parents protested in a letter to a school board member:

> As I mentioned in our meeting, it is of great concern that the District staff recommended that the Board deny our petition without having even returned any of our calls, much less met with us, to discuss any concerns they may have. If they have valid concerns regarding our petitions, they have not been revealed at any time during this eight-month process.

The morning after the school board vote, the Manzanita district superintendent wrote a letter to Community Charter noting that the denial of the charter had been "a very difficult" decision. He went on to say:

> Staff was directed to work with you, if you so desire, to develop your Charter more fully and encourage you to resubmit your charter in the future.
>
> Members of the district office staff would like to set up a meeting with you and other members of your group at your convenience. Please contact me at...

The strong belief that they were justified in their need for an alternative school, coupled with a lack of trust that the school district would treat them fairly, motivated the founders to bypass the district school board and submit their petition directly to the county. They launched a broader public outreach campaign to recruit families across the county and began preparations for a new hearing in six months.

Because the majority of members, even after extensive recruitment, were European American and/or middle class, the potential remained that the charter school could end up serving a predominantly homogeneous, mainstream group of families. A Diversity Statement was drafted in January of 1995, detailing how diversity would be achieved and maintained at the charter school with a target representation of 16% for each of six racial/ethnic groups.[10] This position paper included the following declaration: "If our school cannot find ways to include and reflect all of our communities, it will not open." Nevertheless, Community Charter was still having problems in attracting low-income families to join their group.

In July, a newer Latina member assisted the Diversity Committee in drafting a philosophical statement that laid out more explicitly why the group believed the employment of a quota system was necessary to foster the diversity that they sought. An excerpt follows:

> Because the "isms" are so pervasive in our society, we cannot count on a "first come, first serve" process to provide us with the diverse community the charter school law mandates. Certain groups that have been accustomed to a guaranteed place at the table and take it for granted that they are entitled to a good education for their children will be much more likely to come forward quickly, assume leadership, volunteer their labor and create structures or processes that serve their needs. Groups that have been denied access to resources and power, and whose experiences make them cautious about working in and joining "mixed" groups, will tend to hang back, waiting to see whether the Charter School is in fact committed to and able to meet their needs.
>
> In order to guarantee full participation in the Charter School for all of our communities, we need to consciously create a different process....

Two other new members who were not parents but community activists, Tony and Arthur, were drawn to helping Community Charter after learning of their diversity goals during a public address by one of the founders. They were a gay couple (Asian American and African American/Filipino/Native American mixed race) experienced in community outreach, and they devoted their energies to diversifying the group. The concentrated and persistent efforts of these two men assisted in ethnically diversifying the group profile considerably. The socioeconomic makeup of the membership, however, remained predominantly middle-class and well-educated.

The influx of new members who were willing and able to commit their personal time and resources allowed Community Charter to divide its group energy equally between an aggressive outreach campaign and preparations for the county hearing. The preparations for the hearing were critical, since the planning requested by the county was far more detailed and extensive than the district required. Although the county demands were rigorous, the county superintendent and staff were far more accessible than district personnel: They returned phone calls promptly, answered questions readily, and offered legal information freely. For eight months, the charter group worked to prepare for their hearing before the county board.

In December 1995, the charter petition was unanimously approved by the Warren County Board of Education—approximately one year and eight months after the seven founders held their first organizational meeting.

About the Founders

As the development of the organization progressed, Community Charter gained a small core of approximately eight parents and community members whose participation and dedication matched that of the founders. Some of these participants persevered through the opening of the school. Nevertheless—and not negating these individuals' significant contributions—it appears that the original seven parents formed the nucleus or driving force that kept the vision of Community Charter alive during the petitioning stage of development. The combination of idealism, skills, socio-economic class, education, and political savvy of the founders enabled them to maneuver and overcome chartering hurdles that would possibly have defeated a less educated, less knowledgeable, more marginalized group of parents.

Consider the backgrounds and contributions of five out of the seven founders:

> The father (George) who described himself as having been involved "for the last ten years in radical, political work" was a development director for the local community law center. He not only served as Community Charter's primary grant writer, successfully researching and securing several key start-up grants for the school, but also drafted most of the initial correspondence to the school board and the union. His organizational skills and political know-how, as well as his fund-raising experience, were crucial to the life of the petition drive.
>
> Carl was a lawyer at the same law center as George and moved to the forefront during the charter school's appeal process. Almost all of the legal correspondence from the district and the county concerning the appeal was addressed to him, with response letters drafted and signed by him. Carl researched and wrote a detailed 17-page appeal that was submitted to the county, successfully arguing the case that the local school board acted arbitrarily in denying Community Charter's request.
>
> The one person of color among the founders, Marie, had experience in homeschooling her children, as well as volunteering extensively in a parent cooperative school. Marie took charge of Community Charter's diversity and outreach committee; she was also key to the predominantly European Amer-

> ican group's credibility in low-income communities of color.
>
> In addition to Marie, two other founding mothers—one a preschool teacher and the other a Head Start health coordinator—were instrumental in initially charting and articulating the educational vision and program.

The Community Charter founders were able to draw on their personal resources, contributing skills, training, and in-kind and financial support to overcome the roadblocks thrown in their path by the union and the district. Although they experienced times of frustration and near-defeat ("They [the Manzanita school board, superintendent and staff, and the teachers' union president] treated us so disrespectfully that it was demoralizing") the parents were not intimidated by the system. The dismissal by the district spurred the group on, their socioeconomic and educational backgrounds/status providing the tools to pursue the lengthy, difficult process of appeal. The social and professional network of the Community Charter parents was extensive, providing access to critical information and knowledgeable individuals through phone calls and e-mail. The financial situation of the families and/or the flexibility of the types of jobs they held also allowed them to volunteer an inordinate amount of time to the effort. Nearly all of the start-up expenses prior to December 1995 (estimated at $5,000) were paid by the founders, and their in-kind labor was valued at $25,000. Their economic and *cultural capital* afforded them a resource and knowledge base, confidence in the legitimacy of their mission, a level of ease and authority in arguing their case to the opposition, and the time and energy to sustain a lengthy campaign.[11]

The shared *culture* of the founders also provided an internal framework for group development, communication, and action.[12] All of the parents were friends or acquaintances, or "friends of friends or neighbors." The professional and personal skills, knowledge, and contacts that individual members were able to volunteer were recognized by their colleagues as invaluable to the birth of the charter school. Members appeared comfortable disagreeing openly with one another, and were not embarrassed to cry or express affection in their internal meetings. None of the parents was inhibited in his or her participation by environmental factors that are often associated with poverty, such as transportation problems, concerns about personal safety, or isolation.[13] Although on-site child care was provided at all meetings, interruptions by children were fairly frequent and were treated with a level of patience and understanding that revealed a *likemindedness* in terms of individual parental approaches in dealing with their children, which were nonauthoritarian and child-centered.

At this developmental stage of the organization, after petition approval and before operations begin, all of the founders were congruent in *role conception* and in personality with the *role-demands* of a start-up charter school. All had a prior history of being integrally involved in their children's educations and were familiar with the demands of collective work. Although the members were adamant about having a nonhierarchical organizational structure, personal attributes and skills of individual members shaped their roles/positions in the organization and created an informal hierarchical *social structure*.

For example, George's extensive background in political organizing and development, combined with his willingness and capacity to volunteer an inordinate amount of personal time, created a particularly powerful position for him in the organization. Marie, the only founding member of color, was the key parent in reaching out to communities of color and was therefore crucial to the positive public perception of the mission of the predominantly European American group. As Community Charter evolved and different skills became necessary to move the development of the organization forward, power shifted periodically from member to member. These power shifts were accepted and even welcomed in the small, intimate group. As the membership grew, however, and became more diverse racially and socioeconomically, the power shifts became more problematic.

As mentioned, there were many other members who joined, played major roles for a brief period of time, and then ceased participation abruptly or gradually stopped coming to meetings. Some of the reasons given for ending their involvement included idealistic differences with the core group, job changes, or other commitments that prevented participation, the time-consuming nature of the process, and a belief that the school was never really going to open.

After Petition Approval: Too Much Work

The period between charter approval and actually opening the school doors poses a whole new set of tasks and problems for start-up charter organizers. As witnessed in C-Star's case, visions and broad statements that defined the charter proposal during the petitioning phase must now be made concrete in the design and implementation of the organizational systems and educational program of the school. The nuts-and-bolts interpretation of the mission may not, in its final form, exactly resemble what the founding members originally envisioned. This can cause conflict within a collective group if some members perceive that their individual voices are not being heard. Nevertheless, the necessity to move ahead and get systems in place for operations is paramount.

The minimal "technological and ecological facilities" of Community Charter exacerbated these hurdles, inhibiting action and communication.[14] Individuals were holding committee meetings in parents' homes after work hours or on weekends and there was no office equipment for general use by the membership. Some of the members had access to technology and resources at their individual workplaces, allowing them to function more efficiently on behalf of the organization. Those who did not were unable to produce and contribute equally, which affected their *role-performance* and status in the *social structure* of the group.

The funding of charter schools in general contributes greatly to start-up difficulties. For instance, California state funding for the first seven months of the school year, which is considered to be the period of July through January, is based on the prior-year attendance data of a district's schools. This is problematic for start-up charter schools without a history of enrollment or funding entitlements because it means that they are not eligible to receive state monies until February. This makes it necessary for the new schools to seek outside funding for their planning and early operations stages.[15] Even with the fund-raising expertise and income levels of the Community Charter founders, securing adequate funding for planning was a hardship.[16]

Another problem that charters often experience during this period is that group energy that may have been exhausted during petitioning must be revived, redirected, and/or recruited. The Warren County board had conditioned approval of Community Charter's petition on the timely completion of 16 labor-intensive tasks (i.e., drafting a personnel policy, special education plan, bylaws, enrollment policy, student discipline policy, plan for provision of legal services, and locating a site for operations.) The scope and chilling reality of this work dampened the celebratory mood of Community Charter. Carl illustrated the conflicting emotions of the group on receiving approval:

> Oh shit, now what do we do! ... I was heavily involved during the appeal stuff, to a level I knew I couldn't really sustain timewise. I'm just not going to do that anymore.... There's too much work to be done for it to be done by a few people.

At the general meeting held one month after the county vote, Community Charter drew over 30 participants. The founders were ecstatic; out of these new families, there was bound to be plenty of new energy to assist with all the work that was ahead. Although it was a relief to "pass the baton" to others, the subsequent shift in power from the decision-making control of the tight-knit founding group was not easy. Three incidents during this developmental stage stand out as pivotal moments in the power shift from the founders of Community Charter to the general membership. The conflicts surfaced over three key operational decisions that all start-up charter schools must tackle: defining the organizational structure, setting up a governance system, and choosing a site.

Creating an Organizational Structure

Prior to this first general meeting after the county vote, a small working group, a mix of founders and newer members, met to discuss strategies for meeting the county's conditions and for recruiting and enrolling new families. As a result of this "work party," Tony and Arthur (community members) designed an alternate proposal to replace the interim organizational plan that had already been approved by the larger group. The already approved interim plan did not include paid personnel at this stage of development and was dependent on the labor of the volunteer parent group. Tony and Arthur believed that it was folly to expect volunteers to efficiently tackle the serious amount of work to be done and submitted a detailed, six-page report strongly recommending the hiring of a Communications Coordinator.

At the general meeting, George disagreed with "putting that much power in one person's hands" at that point in time and advocated for a volunteer committee structure. The following is an excerpt of the debate that took place at the meeting:

Tony: [We] would like to put forth a proposal to ensure that the work gets done. There is so much to do and it is vital that we keep abreast of our responsibilities. Now, how do we make sure that everyone knows what's going on? ... Our proposal is for a paid facilitator to be hired to keep things on track and coordinated—

Arthur: A community collaboration facilitator. This person would make sure that we all are connected and informed about what is happening in every part of the group—all committee decisions, outside news we should all know. The key responsibility would be to make sure that the lines of communication are established and kept open.

George: Why a paid position?

Tony: Because this will be a full-time project. It is a vital—an essential component of our organizing process. Our work needs to be coordinated and—

Arthur: This person will have much more responsibility than just making sure information is distributed. They will be our weather vane. Check in with all participants.... The relationships among us are important. We need to rely on someone whose responsibility it is to do this work and if we need to rely on someone that much, we need to pay them....

George: Our original plan was to not concentrate power in one person's hands at this point. We've seen how it's hurt other charter schools when someone—when the power is centralized—

Arthur: It doesn't have to be a negative thing. Access and communication are positive. Lack of information, disconnection—

George: I would rather have a communications committee.

Arthur: This is unrealistic. This feels negative.

[George and Arthur continue debating for another 15 minutes.]

Parent D: Maybe a coordinator would be helpful in keeping everyone informed about committee meetings. This, that is a really hard job. It sounds simple, but as we grow—

Carl: We—I recommend that we not spend more time on this site coordinator because we don't have the money right now. We need to start fund-raising first. Once we start working in committees—

Arthur: I'm personally not satisfied how information flows. It will be a tremendous—tremendous amount of work to do this. It is just too easy for someone to slip out of the loop and—

George: I have strong reservations. I don't know if it's fair to pay one person. I just don't feel good about putting that much power in one person's hands. It scares me. I would rather have a communication committee.

Tony: I think my greatest concern is—perhaps I'm just cynical—but the idea that a group of people will be able to coordinate this? I'm personally concerned.

Carl: I support having a paid person. We have to get the committees working ASAP. Maybe what we need is a concrete proposal to fund this position.

Parent A: Eventually we'll have a paid person, but not now. Maybe we could rely on technology.

Parent B: Could we have the personnel committee address the hiring of a person and set up the communications committee in the meantime?

George: The money, the cost of hiring. We don't have the money.

Tony: Let's not think this way.

George: But it's reality. We have a structure that we've worked on and we haven't—

Arthur: There's too much negative energy about this. The reality is: The amount of work we're doing—People are not going to feel connected.

Parent A: I'm not big on spending money, but I realize that as much work as I'm doing on my committee—But outside my committee, I'm not paying attention to anything outside my committee.

Founder: For most of us to know everything is impossible.

The floor was dominated for over 30 minutes by George and Arthur, and Tony to a lesser degree, forcefully debating their positions. The meeting came to a standstill until Carl reversed his previously voiced support of the idea of having a communications coordinator, and recommended to establish a communications committee instead. The rest of the members then quickly moved to adopt the communications committee recommendation. Although there was some uneasiness voiced about the heated debate erupting between a founder and a newer member, the conflict was viewed primarily by the group as characteristic of the strong male personalities who were involved. One founder thought the incident was more complex and problematic:

> I don't think anyone knows if it would be better or not to have a staff person ... but both of these folks felt so strongly.... At that meeting we had a whole bunch of new people, their first meeting, and it seemed really destructive, and neither of them [George and Arthur] seemed able to say, "No matter how strongly I feel about this, for the greater good, let's just step out and let other people make this decision."

Because the founders possessed the background knowledge that supplied the reasoning for their own decisions, it was hard for George to let go of a policy forged by the founders and allow the newer membership to possibly change the developmental course of the organization. This appeared to be one of the hardest transitions for the founders to make.

The Interim Board

At a meeting one month later, a serious disagreement surfaced about the policy for seating the interim board. Fourteen Community Charter members, including five founders, were present. All the founding members in attendance and some of the newer members supported the institution of a quota system in gender and race in order to ensure the diversity of the governing board. This recommendation was strongly opposed by some of the newer members, particularly Tony and Arthur. The discussion escalated into a heated debate, again dominated primarily by George and Arthur.

George: I think the interim board should reflect who will be our constituency.

Arthur: But we gotta be real. We can't just place people in positions because they meet some exterior criteria.

George: ...We need to think of the future. I know this is hard and maybe not the way we would like to do it, but I'm committed to this being a diverse board and however we need to do that—

Arthur: Quotas? Through quotas? No, no I have to be real. I have a reputation in the community and—

Carl: Well, we have to be real, but we also need to be realistic.

George: Right. And we're not going to achieve the diversity we desire unless we use some sort of mechanism to ensure—

Arthur: If we do this, I just, I just ... It's just so much more complex than having different colored faces on the board... If we do this I can't be a part of this.

[Everyone is silent.]

Tony: This is hard. We're trying to put together something really beautiful, but we are—we're using antiquated methods. These are old tools [quotas] that may not be the best way to achieve what we want.

Arthur: I can't... My reputation in the community—

At the end of the three-hour meeting, the issue was tabled for later discussion and the group left feeling "at odds" and "frustrated." It is interesting to note that the discussion did not fall neatly along racial lines. Eleven members (three African Americans, seven European Americans, and one Latina) were agreeable to using quotas. Tony, Arthur, and one recently joined European American parent were opposed. Although no one was overjoyed about the idea of quotas, the majority agreed that quotas were the only means of achieving the diversity they desired on the interim board. As one parent explained, "They [quotas] don't get us all the way there, but it's a start." In a later conversation, Carl referred to Tony's comment about "using old tools" and remarked:

> We can't put off addressing the issue until we have better tools.... The problem still exists [so] we have to do something. We can't pretend it [racism] doesn't exist...

Another meeting was held the following week, but still no decision on seating the board was reached. A third meeting—facilitated by an outside mediator—was held at which the issue was resolved, but not without difficulty. Eleven parents, including four founders, were in attendance. Tony and Arthur were absent.[17]

In the following excerpt, it is important to reveal the identity of all the participants and their opinions on diversity within the group. To ease identification of individuals' race and gender, all the respondents have been given pseudonyms.

Founders:

George:	European American man
Midge:	European American woman, one of two mothers who recruited the founding group
Marie:	Latina woman, homeschools her children
Donna:	European American lesbian midwife

Newer members:

Bill:	African American man, recently joined
Lena:	European American woman, one of the three members that protested the use of quotas at the prior meeting
Rina:	European American woman, joined during district petitioning period

[The mediator has asked the group members to define the issue that "we are trying to address" in one sentence. This discussion is in process.]

Midge: We want our board to reflect the vision of our school.

Bill: The charter school board should be diverse in every facet.

Donna: But we don't know how we're going to achieve this.

Lena: Everyone agrees with those first two statements, but how do we achieve and define diversity?

George: I have a fear that we don't agree on the vision because of what happened two weeks ago. We may not have agreement on what the vision is for our school.

Rina: There's urgency, though, which changes things—we have this urgency to seat the board.

Donna: Time is an issue.

Mediator: Can someone take a shot at combining all these feelings we've thrown out here into a sentence that will direct our discussion?

[After a bit of brainstorming.]

Donna: How do we swiftly define and achieve diversity for our interim board that reflects the vision of our school?

[Cross-talk. General "oohs" and "aahs" indicating agreement with Donna's summary sentence.]

Marie: Wait a minute. We haven't processed that other meeting yet. At some point we have to do that.

Midge: I'm afraid that the vision of our school is not clear. Diversity is only one part. It was only one [part] of our vision.

Much later in the discussion, an Asian-American father (Joel) made the following comment:

> I think it's fairly well known that I'm not here because of diversity. I know that the primary interest of all of you here is diversity—at least I think it's everyone's primary

> interest, but it's not mine. I'm neutral. I just want a good school for [my child]. I'm here because of the educational opportunity. But I need to ask—Does anyone here know what diversity really means? I want to know why everyone wants diversity? I don't know if you would want it if you really had it.

There were no responses to Joel's comment.

Tension in the room began to mount because it appeared that another meeting would adjourn without seating the interim board. However, in the last fifteen minutes of the three-hour meeting a decision was reached. It seems that the issue was resolved primarily because the group was tired of dealing with it. The policy adopted was that the 15-member board of directors would have a composition of between 10 and 33% representation from each ethnic group in the organization and a gender breakdown of no greater than 40% males.[18] The ethnic and gender composition of the interim board that was actually seated at this time was three African American women, one African American man, one Asian American man, one Latina (Marie), four white women (two of whom were founders), and one white man (George). Four slots remained open to be filled "as quickly as possible, according to the diversity composition decisions already made and those to be discussed in upcoming meetings."

Tony, Arthur, and Lena could not reconcile their opposition to the group's utilization of quotas to achieve diversity on the Community Charter Interim Board and ceased their participation in the group. In a phone conversation with Lena the following day, after seating the interim board, she remarked to me:

> I keep thinking about [Joel's] comment—that we didn't know what real diversity was and that we wouldn't really want it if we had it. Well, what if we had real diversity? What we're doing is not diversity. I bet we all in that room last night went to college. We all come from middle-class backgrounds. This isn't diversity.

The Site

The third critical incident occurred three months later. The interim board was operating fairly smoothly, most of the committees were meeting their deadlines and accomplishing the tasks before them, and enrollment was proceeding as planned. The overall mood was upbeat and the charter school appeared on target to open in four months. Having finally received their official number from the state acknowledging their legal charter status, the only significant hurdle still remaining in Community Charter's path was locating a site for operations.

At first, the Site Committee, which was chaired by founder Midge, confined its search to the more ethnically diverse neighborhoods in the area. After numerous false leads and disappointments, the committee was informed about a vacant building in a predominantly European American, upper-income neighborhood, which was a 20- to 30-minute bus ride from the lower-income communities of color. Although the location appeared contradictory to the diversity goals of the group, the site committee voted unanimously to recommend the building to the interim board, particularly because renovations would be minimal and because "it was already May and there were no other prospects on the horizon." With health and safety regulations to meet, permits to apply for and receive, and furniture and equipment to install before opening, the Site Committee members were in agreement that time was running out. Although the Site Committee voted unanimously to recommend the proposed site, the Outreach Committee unanimously opposed the recommendation, citing the racial and socioeconomic demographics of the neighborhood and the distance from lower-income neighborhoods.

During the interim board discussion, with 15 members in attendance, an emotional and volatile argument erupted after the Site Committee presented its recommendation. In the following excerpt from the meeting, 6 of the participants who were previously identified are indicated by an asterisk:

Founders and members of interim board:
George*: European American man

Midge*: European American woman, chair of Site Committee, one of two mothers who recruited the rest of the initial founding group
Marie*: Latina woman, homeschools her children
Donna*: European American, lesbian midwife

Interim board members:
Bill*: African American man, recently joined
Phyllis: African American woman, joined after approval
Selena: African American woman, joined after approval

General members:
Rina*: European American woman, joined during district petitioning period, member of Outreach Committee
Grace: African American woman, joined after approval, member of Site Committee
Sam: European American man, joined after approval, member of Site Committee
Terri: Puerto Rican/Jewish woman, joined after approval, member of Outreach Committee
Kenneth: European American man, joined after approval, member of Site Committee

[The Site Committee has finished its presentation, unanimously recommending that the group move forward with the proposed location.]

Phyllis: My daughter is now at the Waldorf School, and I find out that it's being moved to [a primarily European American neighborhood]. Well, I am not comfortable with my daughter in that white neighborhood, and I'm certainly not comfortable with us considering putting the school in a rich, white neighborhood.

George: The issue that Phyllis has raised also concerns me—I want the community that surrounds the charter school to be a part of the school. I'm afraid people will look at us and see us as a semi-private school if we locate in an exclusive area.

Terri: My first job was as an assistant gardener in that neighborhood. I only saw Latino people as maids and gardeners and ... I have a deep visceral reaction thinking that our school is going to be there. As a Puerto Rican woman with a Latina daughter, I just can't accept this. If our school had been operating for five years or more and we had a base, I might have said yes, but not now. We're trying to attract people of color to our school. People need to know that we're going to walk our talk. As a member of the Outreach Committee, it's going to be hard to sell this...

Grace: I grew up in [an all African American local community]. I've talked to people all over about our school and they wonder why we're only looking in the [low income neighborhoods]. We should not keep feeding into this stereotype—this reverse racism.

Sam: Everyone should go to the park down the street from the proposed site, it's—

Donna: If we don't go with this site we're not going to have a school. I have a visceral feeling about [the upper income neighborhood], too, but we're talking about a temporary site. The first two years are going to be rocky. We have to get clear about what we need to do here.

Kenneth: I know the area well. I have a lot of experience starting schools. We could have a bus. We're not serving [the upper income neighborhood].

George: That place makes me sick. I don't want to send my kid to an 84% white neighborhood. I don't think this is a last ditch thing—Marie came up with the idea to hold off on this and in the meantime, recruit people from other committees to work on this. I feel we're not in such a desperate position yet. It's, I can't help feeling—I feel like the information the site committee has given is, is sort of like a crowbar.

Selena: I live down the street from [the upper income neighborhood]. I shop there. I go to the park down the street from the [proposed school site] and the only people of color are nannies. Where I live, the people from [wealthy neighborhood] don't want to come down there because we're 70% families of color. I hate to think that I'm going to send my child up that hill.

Grace: Wha—wait a minute. I try to not limit my family. I'm not going to shelter my daughter from—she's in a private, primarily white school and—

Midge: Our presentation was not a crowbar.

Marie: I've worked in [the upper-income neighborhood] for three years at a cooperative preschool, and outreach has just not worked there.

Selena: I'm more concerned about my kids being in that community because they don't have any money.

Kenneth: I feel offended. All of us on the Site Committee wrestled with all of this. Crowbar? I feel offended by this board.... The neighborhood is not our school. If we don't accept this site, are people willing to not open in September?

George: I don't think it's right to say there are no other possibilities.

At this point, Terri broke into tears and accused the Site Committee of completely ignoring the philosophy of diversity that was at the core of the mission. Phyllis and Grace sharply criticized each other's positions. Grace argued that the group should "abandon old fears that lead us to segregate ourselves or feel uncomfortable in different situations," and Phyllis argued that her trust in the group had been seriously undermined by the committee "even considering a site located in that area." The four founders on the board were divided evenly in their positions on the issue, and were visibly shaken by the conflict. By the end of the meeting, even though the decision jeopardized Community Charter's chances of opening in the fall, consensus for the site recommendation was blocked.

The membership was polarized. Parents' opinions and perceptions about the role of diversity in the charter school's mission were at the heart of the disagreement. Some members assumed that diversity would inform all aspects of the school—educational program, admissions, governance, and location. Others believed that diversity was "just one of the principles" in the mission of the school. After three follow-up meetings, including an all-day retreat for the interim board, and numerous phone conversations among the membership, all four African American parents resigned from the board and withdrew from their involvement in Community Charter. Phyllis explained their departure:

> None of us caucused or tried to persuade each other to drop off the board. It was the only thing to do. It made a strong statement, I think. What did it mean to propose that location for the school? What exactly did that mean to me? It meant those people don't have a clue what those words in their documents say. I told [George] that his heart was in the right place but that he needs to start hanging around with some different people.

Midge, one of the two founders who had originally proposed the charter idea to the founding group and who was chair of the Site Committee, also withdrew from her involvement in the organization at this time. In an emotional exchange at a facilitated meeting, she communicated her frustration:

> I feel we are discussing racism and oppression and—these sorts of issues at the expense of education and pedagogy. We did [parent] workshops on diversity but we haven't done any workshops on Reggio. I don't understand [puts hands over eyes and speech is inaudible]... I wasn't the god of the Site Committee! We had a diverse committee that came to a unanimous vote to bring this to the board. You say I have power? I don't have any power. I think I had a place of power when we were five people—

At a meeting less than a month after the volatile site discussion, the general membership decided to delay opening the school for one year. The remaining interim board members voted to dismantle the board and revisit the charter vision before moving forward on any other critical decisions. An excerpt from the public announcement that Community Charter distributed to the membership explaining their decision reads:

> We realized that we have a lot of work to do with each other to arrive at a common understanding of how our commitment to diversity at [Community Charter] will be put in action—how it will come through in our curriculum and in the decision-making structure of our

> group. These issues came to a head in May, when several members of the interim board left, out of frustration at our apparent lack of agreement on the vision...

Developing Trust vs. Moving Forward

As mentioned, while deregulation is a rallying point for charter school proponents, the actual degree of deregulation that characterizes a charter school is dependent on its state law and the sponsor that grants and oversees the charter. The conditions that the county required the Community Charter parents to meet are regulations that are standard fare for most public schools, but they are typically absorbed by the bureaucratic infrastructure. Community Charter's ability as a group to meet these conditions—as far as the array of skills represented by the membership—was quite good compared to many grassroots start-ups. However, the democratic form of decision-making and the nonhierarchical structure that the founders had chosen did not aid the group in moving ahead quickly.

A "collective type" of organizational model, which both C-Star and Community Charter parents envisioned, relies heavily on the development of trust. The time line or time frame for developing a *mutual-benefit* organization should be nonlinear and *organic* to allow for ideas to generate and decisions to be forged through consensus. According to Butler, an important aspect of time in a collective model is the extent to which it allows the atmosphere of mutual trust and common understanding to grow.[19]

Because of the diversity (racial, socioeconomic, geographic) of the families that both charter schools sought to recruit, the development of trust could not be left to chance. As Jean Anyon argues, a "social distance arising in part from lack of mutual experience and knowledge of each other in people of different class and racial backgrounds can impair communication, trust, and joint action."[20] Note the following comment by an African American woman who left the group after the Site Committee issue:

> The kind of work that has to be done here is hard and I don't know if I want to do it with this group. There are

> people who are still comparing their life experience to people of color's experience... I've had a chance to really think about this, and I think that there's nothing wrong with the framework—the structure or systems that the group has worked out. But some of these people—especially the ones that think they know what discrimination is—they have the option of never dealing with racial issues, but I don't.

It appears critical to the realization of founders' initial visions to establish systems that will facilitate relationships among parents and require them to periodically revisit the purpose and values of the organization. Fostering connections among group members based on commitments, not just written contracts, appears to be necessary throughout the planning and operational stages.

The original plan of the Community Charter founders was to mandate, as a requirement for enrollment, that all Community Charter parents and guardians attend workshops on diversity and various community-building strategies. This was attempted during the petitioning stage of development, but the plan was abandoned after the county refused to allow any parental involvement requirements or contracts. Theoretically, it appears that mandated workshops on diversity and conflict resolution would have been extremely beneficial to Community Charter. However, many parents were already overloaded, and the thought of meeting all day for a community-building activity was not welcomed. These workshops also did not appear crucial to the parents in moving things forward, and once again we witness the organizational dilemma of sacrificing principle and purpose for efficiency and expediency.[21] One founder came to realize the value of this type of process work only after attending one of the early workshops:

> The workshops we did in the very beginning were the most useful thing. It was very unifying. I don't mean being lectured at. That kind of stuff is not nearly as useful as when you do participatory stuff.... The most powerful stuff has been when people make themselves

> vulnerable, which results in intimacy.... It involves people kind of revealing a bit about themselves. Finding out that something that I thought was powerful and meaningful is also powerful and meaningful for someone who I thought I didn't have anything in common with is—it makes us closer ... if you had asked me before what will be useful about them [the workshops], I would have said, "I don't know."

The development phase prior to actively petitioning the sponsor—when the *ethos and values* of the school are charted—appears to be conducive to community building and grassroots organizing. An *organic solidarity* can develop through planned group activities that include the children and extended families.[22] However, once formal negotiations are entered into with the sponsor and the community—local unions, neighborhood, and surrounding schools—the chartering experience shifts from a process characterized by a more voluntaristic pacing to one that is more controlled and directed by external rules and demands. Butler has coined the term *strategic time* to identify the organizational experience where the goal is to achieve an outcome in which a "move is followed by a counter move on the part of an opposition, and the next move has to await that counter move" (934). In this stage of the organization's development, parents and community members who come to the table with monetary resources, professional contacts, and pertinent background knowledge or skills in facilitating the work that must be done can create powerful positions for themselves in the *social structur*e. Although these parents' positions of power in the organization are not explicit or formalized, they are very real and can concretely affect relationships among the membership.

For Community Charter, after charter approval the nature of the organizing work and the group experience evolved to yet another stage. Once the reality of a school appeared within reach, a number of new families joined and previous members who had abandoned the group during the district struggle returned. Although the founders and newcomers shared the common goal of opening the school, there was a significant level of incongruence in their thinking about how to reach this goal. For

Community Charter, the absence of formal leadership to coordinate their group efforts during this developmental stage appears to have been a major hindrance to their progress.

There are no guarantees that a designated leader would have solved Community Charter's postpetition/preoperations dilemmas, but it possibly would have provided a means of overseeing and integrating the work of the committees. The informal leadership that the founders provided was not sufficient as the tasks became more complex.

Interim Year and Early Operations

Membership numbers and diversity, participation, and morale plummeted after the announcement of the decision to delay the opening circulated through the group. Five parents who had joined Community Charter just prior to county approval continued their high level of participation and moved into primary roles, replacing three founders who ceased or "put on hold" their involvement. The only participant of color who remained actively involved during this period was founding member Marie.

Later in the summer, a school site, previously a Catholic school, was secured in a low- to middle-income, racially diverse neighborhood (53% African American, 25% white, 10% Asian, 9% Latino, 1% Native American, 2% other ethnicity). Although major renovations were not necessary when Community Charter gained access, the school building was dark and damp inside, and visibly reflected the years of vacancy. The traditional, 1950s-style, institutional facade has concrete steps that lead up from the sidewalk to the heavy double doors of the front entrance. Two fenced-in, concrete, open areas without playground equipment flank the sides of the building.

In order to maintain the lease for the interim year and to help the families who were still integrally involved, the parents decided to organize a small cooperative school at the site. Participation was divided between charter school development work and the interim school, with four parents restricting their involvement to operating the cooperative school. This decision was not without controversy. George explained:

> It's been a real learning experience—what I've learned in just six weeks of this little cooperative school is amazing. Marie has been amazing—a driving force.... It really can act as a laboratory for curriculum, but we really have to be careful and understand and qualify that whatever we develop, we developed in a homogeneous environment.... But we never really sat down and really thought the whole thing through, which we should have. People have come and looked at the little classroom and they see it's all white, middle-income. [One previous Community Charter member] was very upset that we started the interim school because of the lack of diversity. It's also tuition-based because we don't have the funds to do it any other way.... She [the previous member who was upset] is just gone now. She said she didn't want to be involved with us because there were fundamental problems with diversity.

Over the course of the interim year, a variety of in-kind renovation donations by corporate and community sponsors were secured and the small parent group slowly worked to brighten and repair the facilities, starting with the classroom where the interim school was held. Work day schedules were posted in the hallway, detailing the dates for the proposed work, building location of the repairs, the person in charge, and the supplies needed.

During this year, nine other members came to general meetings, off and on, and assisted with various charter tasks (i.e., publicity, county regulations, keeping communication lines open with absent but interested parents, and researching and writing grants). It was not until the following spring that membership numbers and interest began to build. Door-to-door campaigns and open-house activities at the school drew neighborhood families to the school site, and parents began to attend meetings and enroll their children. One particular high note during this year was that George authored and secured a $14,000 start-up grant from the U.S. Department of Education to create a comprehensive and culturally sensitive student assessment system. Community Charter was one of only 16 California schools that were successful in receiving these funds—the first federal charter school monies designated for start-up purposes.

The process of seating a new board of directors began in late April, utilizing the policy previously developed by the group to ensure race and gender balance. The turmoil that had characterized the previous year's process did not reoccur. Three of the five remaining founders assumed board positions, two slots were filled by county representatives, three by community members (without children enrolled in the charter school), and the remainder by new parents. Donna, an African American/Native American computer analyst and mother of a K/1 student, was elected board chair. Donna did not live in the immediate neighborhood and had found out about Community Charter from parents at the Montessori school where her child was previously enrolled.

A full-time education coordinator (a European American woman) and a 2/3/4 teacher (a European American man) were the first staff hired. Both had experience in charter schools: The coordinator had previously worked as a teacher in a local start-up, and the 2/3/4 teacher was a C-Star parent who had served on the second-year C-Star board of directors. Other Community Charter administrative staff included a half-time site coordinator (an African American woman) and a half-time community coordinator (an African American man.) The last two credentialed teachers for the two K/1 classrooms (an African American woman; a European American man) were not hired until two weeks before school started. Both were unseasoned teachers and unfamiliar with charter schools. An on-site extended day care program was added to the school offerings, with all staffing and administrative costs to be generated by fees paid by parents.

On September 2, 1997, the charter school opened with an enrollment of 64 children (29% African American, 29% multiracial, 24% white, 12% Latino/Hispanic, 6% Asian). Although there was still some renovation work in progress, the school office and classrooms were ready for operations, fully furnished and stocked with office equipment, instructional materials, toys, books, and art supplies. Television crews and newspaper reporters were on site to capture the emotions and excitement. Founding parents and those who had persevered through the interim year were in tears as the children streamed in the doors that first day.

The First Six Months of Charter Operations

Some of the problems that surfaced and themes that emerged in Community Charter's first six months echoed C-Star's operational experience. There were difficulties in the recruitment of experienced teachers and in the mentoring of new teachers. There were also multiple problems in the areas of health and safety regulations, insurance, special education, and payroll.

Within two weeks of opening, Community Charter lost students and some involved parents as a result of a novice teacher. A particularly hard blow for the parents who had been involved for the past two to three years was that Carl removed his child from the school during this time. Although Carl cited a number of reasons for the decision, many parents believed that it was because Carl didn't want his son in the classroom of an inexperienced teacher. This created hard feelings among some of the founders. Carl explained, however, that there were multiple reasons for his family's decision:

> During the interim year a number of important things happened in the district: class sizes were reduced in the lower grades and multi-age/grade classrooms became available ... We also were going through some tough family stuff at the time and we just couldn't keep up with the toll that [Community Charter] was taking out of our lives. A brand new, inexperienced teacher was not the only reason we left—a lot of people thought it was and very few people took the time to actually ask us. There were so many things that needed attention at the school—the fire marshall was on our case and threatening to shut us down, we had problems with the insurance, problems with payroll—so many crises that were constantly threatening to be showstoppers. There was just so much that needed attention and we [my family] knew we just couldn't keep up with the level of

> intensity. I guess some folks felt betrayed by our decision, but—

Carl remained on the Community Charter board, but his involvement and commitment dropped considerably after this.

Another major problem for Community Charter was the lack of involvement of approximately 60% of the parents/guardians. The sponsor's refusal to allow Community Charter to require a minimum level of parent/guardian involvement as a criterion for enrollment appears to have contributed to this situation. The need to rebuild enrollment numbers that declined as a result of the postponement was also cited by founders and other actively involved parents as a contributing factor. New parents enrolled their children but did not participate in an orientation about the mission and goals of the organization.

Even though Community Charter had the extra year to plan and prepare for the opening of their school, the postponement resulted in the loss of a large number of families who were oriented to the parent involvement mission. As one parent (an actively involved member of the group before petition approval) explained:

> I don't think we ever rebuilt the base. There was a lot of scrambling to build numbers. It feels like we never got back to where we were ... it doesn't feel as cohesive. There were a lot of times we wondered during that year [interim year] if it was really going to happen. We were scared to be hopeful. It wasn't until midsummer when we felt it was really going to happen.

A large number of the new parents and guardians were happy to have a small, family-oriented neighborhood school and were enrolling for that reason instead of the parent involvement policy or the educational program. Note the following explanations from new parents—all African American, but of different family income levels—on why they enrolled their children in Community Charter:

> I wanted to save the money I was spending on my child's monthly education. I was interested for purely selfish reasons.

> It's small. Close [to the family's home] and teachers seem nice.
> [At this point, I asked for her opinion about the school's mission and its influence on her choice. She replied:]
> It's okay... everyone is friendly.

> I like their attitude. I walked up here one day to see what was going on and they were all outside—kind of getting people—attracting them to look at what they were doing for kids and I liked that. [My son] said someone even came to our apartment to tell me about it [the charter school].

An estimate given by parents about overall parent involvement at the charter school ranged from 10–20% very involved, 20–30% minimally involved, and 50–60% not involved. Of the 50–60% uninvolved parents, George estimated that 20% "don't know what's going on at all." As the school year progressed, those parents who continued to assume responsibility on a daily basis and participate in the decision making were—except for the board of directors chair—from the same core group who were involved in the years prior to operations.

The third challenge for Community Charter that emerged in the first six months was the supervision of administrative staff. Although the Community Charter administrators were not directors of the organization and were hired by the parents to implement a program conceived by the parents, supervision and holding staff accountable were problematic. The experience with the community coordinator is a good example of the staff accountability dilemma.

The community coordinator's primary job was to act as the parent liaison to facilitate two-way communication, to elicit parent participation in school activities, and to further develop the parent involvement policy. This position was particularly important due to the sponsor's refusal to allow a parent/guardian involvement requirement as a condition of enrollment. The parents who were recruiting and interviewing staff were very much aware of the need for an individual who could work effectively with and be a bridge to the families of color who were the majority of Community Charter's enrolled population. During the time period when the parents were hiring, Marie met Ray, an African American political activist with a well-respected and lengthy history in the local community. Marie brought the news back to the group that Ray was interested in becoming involved in the school. As a result, Community Charter recruited Ray for the half-time community coordinator position. Of the three administrative positions, this was the only one without a job description.

When I asked Ray about the *role-requirements* of his position during an interview in October, he explained:

> I am here to meet the individual needs of parents and children. If a student needs individual attention in reading or math, I can supply this. I am also the community liaison and I contact outside businesses for volunteer opportunities, supplies. I bring in outside performing artists. I try to get more parent involvement. My major challenge is, since we are a diverse school, is to balance differences so we won't pull each other apart. My role is to demand that all sit at the table with a willingness to learn and grow. There are cultural differences. There are parents who have special concerns. Black folks want discipline. [This is] a difficult reality for the [middle-class] white child. We have to consider these differences and not assume we know why.... So far it's a miracle. I'm pleased with the willingness of everyone to work.

Ray spoke positively about Community Charter's vision and his opportunity to play a role in the implementation of the mission; however, he did not offer concrete proposals or strategies for eliciting parent participation/involvement.

In a January interview, although hopeful and upbeat, one of the working core of parents expressed her disappointment at the low percentage of parents who were integrally involved in the school and added, "We were hoping that Ray was going to take a more active role in parent coordination." The disjuncture between the parents' hopes and vision of how the community coordinator was going to carry out his job and Ray's *role-conception/performance* was not easily resolved and grew to be a source of tension as the year progressed. Toward the end of the school year, Ray began to spend less time at the school—sometimes missing work without informing the education coordinator—and eventually resigned from his position.

At the end of this first school year, the parents formed a restructuring committee to address the first-year problems. The committee was led by founder Donna, and the key data-gatherers and decision-makers of the committee were parents from the pre-operations core working group. One of the newer African American Community Charter parents remarked that she was not pleased with this committee because it was

> a lot of the same people that do everything—that same group. They're all white except for one or two people. But that's not what bugs me—what bugs me is not that they're white, but that it's the same people who if you disagree with them they take offense. And it's their kids that other parents complain about as having no manners and acting out with the teachers…

As far as staff turnover going into the second year was concerned, one teacher, the educational coordinator, and the community coordinator chose not to return. The resignation of the educational coordinator prompted the decision to adopt a more traditional administrative structure and hire a director/principal, an office manager, and a site coordinator. Parent involvement was designated as a primary responsibility of the director/principal.

Barriers

The Community Charter founders believed they were prepared for the difficulties they would encounter in their initial year of operations, but as George explained:

> We didn't know it would be this hard. I knew the first year would be crazy, but not the kind of crazy it is.

It would seem that the additional year to regroup, secure outside start-up funding, and further develop systems and procedures would soften or alleviate some of the operational challenges for a start-up charter school. However, a combination of external and internal factors appear to have laid the groundwork for a difficult start-up for Community Charter regardless of the additional time.

An obvious barrier to the founding process was the lack of start-up funding. Insufficient start-up capital can impact who becomes and remains involved in charters—during the early founding phase as well as the development stage closer to operations. It also plays a role in the conditions of the facility and how well children and families are served.[23]

As witnessed in both case studies, the lack of start-up funds translated into not being able to hire staff during the critical development phase to plan as a team and/or having to require those who were "hired" earlier on to work without pay. Last minute hiring severely limited the pool of effective, experienced teachers that applied for positions. Inexperienced teachers enter the field with varying degrees of talent and skill, and they evolve and improve through managing their own classroom, professional development, and a supportive work environment. Unfortunately, in the case of small start-up charter schools, there may be minimal opportunities for teacher mentoring and professional assistance for the novice in the classroom.

Over 60% of start-ups, 34.6% preexisting public schools, and 52.7% of private conversion charter schools across the nation cite the lack of start-up funds as a major barrier to development and implementation.[24] Ron Corwin, Lisa Carlos, Bart Lagomarsino, and Roger Scott reported in their technical paper to the San Diego Unified School Board in 1996,

> The charter school legislation in California, by not including start-up funds to provide support and training to those starting up a school, seems not to acknowledge the skills and resources such a task requires—an

> undertaking that has often been described as being more difficult than starting a new business.[25]

Another external hurdle in Community Charter's case was the sponsor's disallowance of a parent involvement requirement as a basis for enrollment. Considering the inherent problem of maintaining internal democratic processes in a *mutual-benefit association*, not having an enforceable requirement would appear to have greatly inhibited Community Charter's chances of realizing their founding vision of a parent-run, democratically managed school with a heterogeneous membership. Perhaps this part of the vision should have been revisited and substantially altered by the charter school working group after charter approval. Leaving such an integral component of the operating structure in the hands of a half-time employee—without a job description, with no experience in this area, and with no agreement as to how he would approach the task—was not, in hindsight, a smart decision.

As mentioned earlier in this case study, it appears that a director, coordinator, or principal hired immediately following charter approval would have substantially aided Community Charter's development. An experienced school administrator could possibly have directed and integrated the valuable energies of the core group of parents and community members immediately after charter approval and prevented the derailment of the opening. The daily presence and focused energy of a full-time educational leader after operations could have assisted in keeping staff on track and provided the mentorship necessary for novice teachers. Of course, hiring a leader is not a guarantee that everything will proceed without conflicts or problems. However, the crucial integration and overseeing of complex tasks in the post-approval through operations phases of a charter school's development appears to demand that one or a few individuals "have the authority—the legitimate right—to make demands, exert influence, and impose sanctions."[26] As witnessed in the C-Star case study, however, processes must be in place for the membership to hold leaders accountable.

The fact that parents will be supervising or evaluating the performance of the charter school's leader should indicate to both parents and prospective employees that a "status quo" educational administrator may not be an appropriate choice for the position. Sarason clearly emphasizes that educators have always recognized that parents have a legitimate vested interest in what happens in schools; nevertheless, this does not mean educators believe "that interest should be formally accompanied by the power to influence how schools and classrooms are structured and run, the choice of curriculum, (or the) selection of teachers and other personnel."[27] A system where parents are empowered by mandate to hold their educational leaders accountable is a radical shift from traditional public school operations.

Another critical concern is this: Would the Community Charter founders have had the capacity to "let go" and allow a hired director to lead the organization to its next plateau? A dedicated, persevering founding group of parents can be a start-up's greatest asset, as well as its biggest problem. The stages through which a grassroots charter school evolves are not finite or neatly bound with markers for parents that indicate when to "Yield," "Merge," or "Back off." The concept of parents as equal partners in public schools requires a fundamental shift in the thinking not only of professional educators, but of parents as well.

Taking into account some of the internal dilemmas that appear to be inherent in a collective-like or *mutual-benefit* organizational structure, as well as the external barriers that face grassroots charter schools in general, the final discussion that follows explores some possible avenues that founders and charter advocates might pursue in re-visioning a parent-run charter school.

NOTES

1. Key to symbols used in quotations:
   Three dots (...) indicate omission of words within a sentence.
   Four dots (....) indicate omission of complete sentence(s).
   Dashes (—) between words indicate connections or clarifications of trains of thought.
   Dashes (—) at the end of a block of text indicate respondent's intention of continuing to speak.

2. *Ethos and values:* Vision; deep beliefs. The following are some of the questions that frame the National Study of Charter Schools' investigation of *ethos and values* in field sample charter schools. The questions reveal the foundational role that *ethos and values* can play in the mission and educational program of a charter school.
   - What are the distinguishing characteristics of the guiding beliefs and how coherent and shared are they?
   - How does the school staff describe the school's vision? How do parents? Students?
   - How important is the vision/mission in the everyday life of the school?
   - How coherently is the vision being implemented?
   - Have important elements of the vision/mission of the school become modified over time? Is so, how and why?

   (From RPP International's Field Brief Guide for the National Study of Charter Schools, 1997.)

3. The National Study reports that a key motivator for founding a charter school—cited by three out of four charter schools—is the implementation of an alternative educational vision that is not possible within the traditional public system. Almost six out of ten charter schools surveyed reported it to be the most important reason for becoming a charter school. RPP International, 1999.

4. Dianda and Corwin, *Vision and Reality*.

5. Although the California Board of Education eventually moved to approve waivers to grant additional charters in February 1996, this outcome was unknown during Community Charter's petitioning process. In 1998, the statewide cap was raised to 250 charter schools for the 1998–99 school year. An additional 100 schools can be authorized each year after that. The original district cap of 10 charter schools was also eliminated at this time.

6. Becker, Nakagawa, and Corwin, *Parent Involvement Contracts in California's Charter Schools*.

7. The 1992 California charter law required that a charter petition must be signed by no fewer than 10% of the teachers currently employed in the local district school, or by no fewer than 50% of the teachers employed at one school in the district. This state requirement was abolished for start-ups in the 1998 charter legislative changes.

8. The original California charter law allowed charter schools to hire non-credentialed teachers. The 1998 revisions specify that teachers must be certified.

9. Under the 1998 revision of the California law, charter petitioners can apply directly to their county board of education, and, if denied, they can then apply to the state board of education. The original law restricted sponsorship to the charter group's local school board, and only after being denied could the charter group appeal to the county board.

10. The Community Charter position statement outlined the following: "Diversity in race and ethnicity will be obtained through the use of enrollment pools for the following six groups: African American, Asian American, European American (including Jewish ethnic group), Latina/Latino, Multi-racial/Mixed Heritage, and Other Ethnicities. [Community Charter] will strive to create a student body and group of participating adults with equal proportions (16%) in each of these six racial/ethnic groups, and will ensure that

each group has no less than 10% and no greater than 25% representation in the School."

The position statement also included an explanation of why the group believed employing a quota system was warranted: "We want our children to know and be close to children and adults of cultures, social classes, sexual orientations, family structures, physical abilities, first languages, occupations, religions, or spiritual practices and ways of thinking that differ from their own and those of their families... Although we are uncomfortable with the idea of sorting children by percentages or other forms of quota systems in order to produce the learning community we desire, we refuse to adopt a 'color blind' approach that could result in a homogeneous population."

11. Bourdieu, "Cultural Reproduction"; Smrekar, *Impact of School Choice*; and Lareau, *Home Advantage*.

12. *Culture.* Core values, assumptions, and beliefs that provide a framework for group development and action. The *social structure* of an organization or working group "tends to reflect underlying cultural values and helps to realize those values. *Culture* and *social structure* tend to be relatively congruent." However, the degree of congruence can be tenuous in a new organization. "Over time, changes in the one are likely to produce changes in the other." Newton and Levinson, "The Work Group," 130–31.

13. Smrekar, *Impact of School Choice.*

14. Levinson, "Roles, Personality, and Social Structure."

15. As of August 1999, the California Department of Education plans to provide "advance apportionment" funds to charter schools for those students who were previously enrolled in public schools. "Charter schools serving students who were not previously enrolled in the public schools may have to wait until February to begin receiving the state funds for such students." The new funding bill, AB 1115, does not

clarify how start-up charter schools will be funded nor does it specify whether charter school funding should follow the existing advance apportionment rule. From Eric Premack, *1999 Preliminary Overview*.

16. The original California charter school funding model made no provisions for start-up funding. A loan system for charter schools was subsequently enacted, but it limited loans to a maximum of $50,000, to be repaid within two years, and required that a school district apply on behalf of a charter school. Much of the loan fund remained untapped because of the low cap, and many school districts would not apply for loans on behalf of charter schools.

    Senate Bill 267, which allows charter schools to apply directly to the California Department of Education for start-up loans, was passed during the 1999–2000 legislative session. This fund contains over $5 million in combined state and federal charter loan funds and is available to start-up (non-conversion) charter schools. This bill increases the loan cap to $250,000 and expands the maximum repayment period to five years. From Eric Premack, *1999 Preliminary Overview*.

17. Tony and Arthur did not attend another general meeting. However, they continued their work on the Outreach Committee for a short time before dropping out of the group altogether. Shortly after their departure, the two began working on the organization of another local start-up charter school.

18. The suggestion of limiting participation of the males to 40% was posed by founder Donna, who believed that the men in the group often dominated and set the tone of the meeting discussions. She offered at a later meeting to drop this suggestion in order to move the process along, but the rest of the group voted to keep it.

19. *Organic time*. Butler alludes to the natural growth of plants to highlight "the need to tend to the general environment of

processes, through feeding and nourishing, rather than through direction and control." Butler, "Time in Organizations," 930.

20. Jean Anyon, "Race, Social Class, and Educational Reform in an Inner City School," *Teachers College Record* 97.1 (1995): 69–94, 76.

21. Sarason, *Parental Involvement*.

22. Butler, "Time in Organizations."

23. See above note 16.

24. RPP, *Charter Schools*, 1999.

25. Ronald G. Corwin, Lisa Carlos, Bart Lagomarsino, and Roger Scott, "From Paper to Practice: Challenges Facing a California Charter School," Executive Summary (San Francisco: WestEd, May, 1996), 13.

26. Newton and Levinson, "The Work Group," 126.

27. Sarason, *Parental Involvement*, 20.

CHAPTER FIVE

DECISION MAKING, VISION, & COMMUNITY BUILDING

The National Study of Charter Schools identifies a number of key barriers that commonly face founders in the development and implementation of charter schools. At the top of the list are lack of start-up funds (54.7%); inadequate operating funds (41.4%); inadequate facilities (35.8%); lack of planning time (37.4%); state or local board opposition (20.7%); district resistance or regulations (19.9%); and internal conflicts (14.2%).[1]

Mediating External Barriers

In both case studies in this book, the ability to surmount obstacles was influenced by founders' educational and economic backgrounds, work experiences, and social and professional networks. It appears that parents who are professionals and/or have higher levels of education have an advantage in that their social and cultural capital provides a foundation for grasping the implications of the state charter law and the regulations for implementation on charter practice. Family, friends, and work associates link them casually and professionally with valuable contacts and resources in the local community, as well as on the state and national levels. Upper/middle socioeconomic backgrounds and professional livelihoods, however, are not prescriptions for bypassing difficulties. And as witnessed in C-Star's case, neither is partnering with an experienced educator a guarantee for a smooth founding experience.

For parents to enhance their charter group's ability to overcome the hurdles that appear inherent in the founding process (i.e., start-up funding, inadequate operating funds, and political opposition), one suggestion is to seek a partnership with an established, local community nonprofit prior to petitioning the sponsor. A partnership with an organization that has an established track record in the community could enable charter founders to secure loans for start-up and provide some local political support for their venture. Of course, the potential partner would have to be carefully researched before being approached to establish not only its financial viability and reputation, but also whether or not the partner organizations are congruent as far as mission and goals. The charter school's degree of autonomy would be dependent on the details of the legal partnership that is forged between the organizations; therefore, founding parents would have to be very clear about their school's mission as well as the type of business relationship they wish to establish. The founders should also clarify among themselves exactly what it is they wish to gain from partnering with a particular organization.

There are some interesting examples in Texas of charter founders in partnership with various types of organizations such as community nonprofits, universities, and private schools. It is a requirement of the Texas law that charter founders partner with established organizations. The degree of autonomy varies with the types of business relationships that founders legally establish with their partners at the outset. In two of the Texas charter schools I visited as a researcher for the National Study—both schools serving predominantly Latino, low-income families—each charter outlined a very different relationship with its partner. One, an elementary school, operates completely autonomously, having used its partner primarily for start-up stability. The other, a middle school, operates as one of many community programs under the partner organization's jurisdiction. It appears that Texas policymakers gained from the experiences of the first charter states, who witnessed grassroots start-ups limping through their first years on minimal funding and politically rough terrain.

The third most problematic barrier cited in starting charter schools across the country is the challenge of securing/renovating/maintaining adequate facilities. Our two case studies had very different experiences in this area, but for both groups the issue of the school site consumed parent energies and seriously threatened the beginning of operations. In C-Star's case, projected expenditures in their first-year budget did not include paying rent for a facility—a verbal agreement, forged initially with the district, was later reversed. In addition to the poor condition of the building the district eventually secured for C-Star, the identified location was a neighborhood far from the founding and first-year families. This decision played a primary role in the demographic shift of the school community in just one year; from a heterogeneous racial and socioeconomic mix of families to a more homogeneous population (white, middle-class).

Considering C-Star's demographic changes after the first year, Community Charter's decision to pass on a potential school site located in an upper-income neighborhood appears to have been a wise move. The internal conflict that erupted over the Community Charter decision was unfortunate; however, without a provision for transportation funds in the California state charter law, the distance of the school from low-income neighborhoods could have seriously impacted the diversity goals of Community Charter's founding vision. Foreseeing some of the implications the location and physical plant can have over time on a charter school's founding vision could save operators from sweating over student turnover, recruitment, major restructuring of the educational program, or relocation during the critical first years of operation.

Creating and Maintaining the Founding Vision

This leads us to an area that merits further discussion: the critical importance of charting a founding vision that will assist in guiding decision making and operations, rather than act as a barrier. The interplay of external factors and a charter's founding vision appears to be an ongoing dance in the life of a charter school. It seems critical for charter founders to come to grips early on with the fact that "circumstances change."[2] Political context, neighborhood demographics, personnel, and student population are just some of the factors that can change over time. In addressing this interplay among external factors, internal changes, and the founding vision, how do organizers and operators maintain or remain true to the fundamental reason or educational philosophy for founding their charter school in the first place?

An obvious suggestion is for founders, in charting the vision, to carefully distinguish the primary components of their founding vision from secondary or supporting elements. This may seem elementary, but in both of the case study schools, the source of much of the early internal conflict was centered around the vision and the various interpretations of the "core vision." For example, the C-Star parents believed that the parent "collective" or "co-op" was part of their charter school's vision; but it was never really discussed in depth as a group by the founders. Their leader believed "the cooperative idea" to be just that, "just an idea." In Community Charter's case, the issue of diversity was viewed by some as just one of many elements in their vision; for others in the founding group, it was the nucleus. The problems inherent in articulating a founding vision (C-Star), or in prioritizing and problematizing elements of the vision (Community Charter) were not visible to the parents when their charters were being drafted.

During this *organic* organizational stage, it appears that decision making through consensus building proceeded smoothly because of the *likemindedness* that was perceived among group members. Motivation to abandon the traditional public school system was strong enough to provide the glue for forming a "community" at this stage of the charter's development. "Decisions about the future [were] made by judgment and 'satisficing' proceeding upon the acceptance of satisfactory solutions rather than searching until an optimal solution [was] found."[3]

A decision-making strategy that may be helpful for founding charter groups to employ during this early period is Karl Weick's *retrospective sense-making,* or "thinking in the future perfect tense."[4] Future perfect thinking is an exercise that Weick proposes for organizational managers when speculating about the future effects of a present decision. His argument is:

> If one is able to treat a future event as if it's already over and done, then presumably it's easier to write a specific history based on past experience that could generate that specific outcome. The future event is more sensible because you can visualize at least one prior set of means that will produce it. The meaning of that end *is* [his emphasis] those means that bring it about.[5]

Engaging in detailed discussions about the charter school's future "as though it were already part of an unfolding past" could be a powerful exercise for charter founders. Locating the school in various futures and discussing the events that led to specific outcomes could possibly assist in separating the core components of the vision from strategies for implementation that could be altered depending on external circumstances. If nothing else, the discussions/brainstorming could be a critical exercise that might facilitate the founders' view of the charter school as an entity separate from themselves with a future of its own. Eugene Bardach explains that

> [talking] about the present as though it were an omen about the future serves a critical function. It is a shorthand way of making sense out of what a heterogeneous community is collectively doing. It is a way for the group to develop a self-consciousness about their ability to act meaningfully in a disorderly world.[6]

Building Community

Retrospective sense-making could also be employed as an aid in decision making when an organization enters a *spasmodic* timeframe, such as the phase of a start-up charter's development that immediately follows petition approval.[7] This is a crucial time, when new families are joining; location/renovation/preparation of the site is taking place; operating systems and procedures are being drafted; personnel are being recruited and hired. Decision making during this time can be opportunistic or rash in order to move the process forward. The democratic process can seem interminably slow, which promotes the group acceptance of one or two members taking hold of a situation and moving things along. This acceptance of one person or a small group assuming decision-making control does not necessarily mean that the majority of members are apathetic, but could result from the lack of background experience among most parents of knowing how to participate in the process. *Retrospective sense-making* may not necessarily guarantee the effectiveness of decisions, but it can spark creativity and innovation in reaching solutions during a period of uncertainty.[8] It could also serve as a means of bringing new members into the center of the decision-making circle, as well as a conscious strategy for building community.

For example, when C-Star's bylaws were being framed, *retrospective sense-making* could have been a means for parents and staff to understand and absorb the implications of a hierarchical governance structure. Concretizing the concept of governance into future perfect scenarios centering around staff accountability or educational program evaluation could serve to educate average laypeople—unfamiliar with how the rules and goals of the larger structure affect everyday relationships—and offer them a way of participating meaningfully in discussions that would chart policy for school operations.

What also comes to mind is Community Charter's period immediately following charter approval, when the organization experienced a dramatic increase in attendance at general meetings. Although the founders were excited about the potential new members and heartily welcomed their participation, there was no strategy—except for introductions at the beginning of meetings and the orientations—to facilitate new members' entry into the "inner circle." The orientations served as an exchange of information, but usually this communication was one-way: from old members to new potential members. New members asked questions, offered information on what they could contribute to the charter school (work experience, interest, contacts, etc.), and explained the educational needs of their families (number of children to be enrolled, their special educational or behavioral needs, etc.). In discussions that involved the entire group at general meetings, only a very small number of key players consistently engaged in the floor debates. Those members whose ideas dominated the decision making were skilled in public debate and/or more knowledgeable than others about the history of Community Charter. The majority seemed to be agreeable to allowing those few members to control the direction and content of the debate; however, from this period through the first year, a recurring theme across interviews and conversations with newer parents was their disgruntled feeling of "not being a part of the core group." Although the core group (founders and others integrally involved prior to operations) lamented the minimal involvement on the part of other parents, there was the perception among newer parents that their opinions, if different from those of the core group, were not welcomed and would not be heard.

The idea of building a charter school community governed collectively by parents should not be idealized or used loosely as a mere marketing tool to attract families. Underestimating the importance of defining "parent-run" or "parent co-op" early on appears to be a setup for internal conflict. Thoughtful statements championing the ideas of "community" and "parent involvement" framed the charter petition, new articles, and public announcements of C-Star, but few concrete strategies were outlined for actually building the "communities" that the school sought.

Community Charter, however, put countless hours into creating and outlining an organizational structure that placed parents in chief governing roles, but at the end of their first year of operations, only about 15% were highly involved. Most of the low-income parents/guardians of color from the immediate neighborhood were involved minimally or not involved at all. Reaching out, educating, including new members in charter school operations, and increasing opportunities for face-to-face deliberations among parents should not be among the many duties of a half-time coordinator or a volunteer committee. It seems critical that parents take time to search for, and screen rigorously and thoughtfully, all candidates for staff positions. As we witnessed with both C-Star and Community Charter, this is very difficult to do without start-up funding.

Parent Requirements as a Condition of Enrollment?

Considering the demands on families' lives today, as well as the difficulties educators cite in eliciting parent involvement in schools, it seems likely that a parent-run charter school would not have wide appeal. However, because of the more visible positive factors—such as the location or the small size of a charter school—parents and guardians enroll their children regardless of parent involvement clauses. Until more public school choices are available to middle- and low-income families, this is a reality that must be considered.

Establishing parent involvement requirements as a condition of enrollment appears to be the most logical answer to this dilemma. This would not automatically solve all the problems of maintaining internal democracy, but it would provide a foundation for a *mutual-benefit* type of organizational structure on which to build. Without an enforceable contract, it seems that chances are just too great for unequal participation to create factions among parents (for example, C-Star's second year), which periodically cause internal conflicts that threaten the school's stability and ability to meet its obligation of educating students. However, as seen in the cases of two neighboring charter schools, the decision to adopt enforceable parent contracts does not rest solely with the founders or the state law, but also with local school boards and sponsors.

Nevertheless, even with parent involvement contracts in place, it appears likely that the dilemma of internal democracy will be an ongoing concern. Finding multiple ways for new parents to participate meaningfully and have a voice equal to founding parents in the charter school is an ongoing challenge that does not decrease over time. Founding parents can sometimes contribute to the problem by appearing cliquish to parents outside of the founding circle. Founding parents can also feel responsible for every aspect of the school and want to be involved in all decisions, to the dismay of staff. Needless to say, placing parent involvement at the center of a charter school's mission is a decision that must be thoughtfully considered and realistically approached. Understanding the importance of establishing an organizational structure, governance system, and supporting policies that facilitate a parent involvement mission, rather than act as barriers is a first step.

A Parent Learning Community

> Authentic community requires us to do more than pepper our language with the word "community," label ourselves as a community in our mission statement, and organize teachers into teams and schools into families. It requires us to think community, believe in community, and practice community.[9]

In charter schools that are attempting to adopt or adapt a *mutual-benefit* type of association, where parents chart policy and make decisions collectively for the organization, it is critical for charter founders and sponsors to identify and establish a means for the charter school membership to learn how to participate, make decisions, govern, and assess their performance in fulfilling public education interests. "Community building," "building trust," "building consensus," and "governing collectively" are all terms that are found repeatedly throughout the Community Charter and C-Star transcripts, but the strategies for implementation fall short of achieving and nurturing the organizations that each school desired. Founders' romanticization of the concept of "community" was detrimental to the viability of both charter school organizations.

Considering Sergiovanni's quote above about "authentic community," how can a parent-run charter school "practice community" without threatening the life and overall purpose of the organization? This question is particularly critical because charter schools as public education institutions are *commonweal* organizations whose stakeholders encompass the public at large. In the cases of C-Star and Community Charter, the time and attention paid to maintaining internal democracy and collective governance concerns impacted each school's performance in educating its students. And what would prevent charter groups from using methods such as parent contracts as exclusionary strategies to filter out families who do not share the cultural values or religious beliefs of the majority?

If grassroots, collectively organized and governed public schools are allowed under a state charter law, then sponsors and charter advocates must seriously contemplate how this charter school model might operate and succeed, while reinforcing democratic values. The appeal of "school-as-community" appears to be a strong one, drawing parents and guardians from all political persuasions, religious backgrounds, and ethnic groups. But because of the overall lack of collective opportunities for adult citizens to reason and make decisions together, it seems likely that most parents—across income groups and social sets—would not have vast experience to draw from to guide them in their participation.

Charter researcher and education professor Stacy Smith argues that charter schools are in need of normative standards that can be utilized to balance particularistic aims against public interests, and she sees the reform movement "as an opportunity to reflect upon the tenacious dilemma of liberal versus communitarian visions of democratic public life."[10] Smith proposes a model of democratic association for charter schools that addresses "how they are to fulfill their peculiarly public functions—governing themselves and reproducing democratic citizenry" (137). She draws from two strands of deliberative democratic theory—Seyla Benhabib's "participationism" and Joshua Cohen's "strategy of associative democracy"—to ground her argument:

> Taken together, Benhabib's participatory vision and Cohen's associative strategy provide a model of democratic politics that closely reflects the organizational structure of multiple, distinct charter schools within the public educational sphere. Charters are autonomous public associations concerned with addressing common educational interests. Charter schools are public institutions, yet they are granted regulatory relief from direct state control. Thus, the deliberative model of democratic politics would view charters as "arenas for public deliberation that lie outside conventional political arenas."[11]

According to Smith, Benhabib's "participationism" is rooted in Habermas's discourse theory of deliberative democracy, which mines the strengths of liberalism and civic republicanism, yet discards their weaknesses. Political participation and democratic decision making are emphasized; and the civic republican desire for shared ethical life and corresponding assimilative tendencies are rejected. In Benhabib's model, "the public sentiment which is encouraged is not reconciliation and harmony, but rather political agency and efficacy, namely the sense that we define our lives together, and that what one does makes a difference."[12]

As deregulated public schools of choice, charter schools provide a unique opportunity for heterogeneous groups of individuals to organize around and participate in shared concerns. The communities that are formed are not dependent on homogeneity in cultural values or ethnicity, and the public spaces created encourage face-to-face deliberation. Smith utilizes Cohen's work to point out that these types of associations are of great benefit to the society at large because they provide forums for public deliberation that are not located within the conventional political arena. Because of their "outsider" location, these associations can provide public spaces for addressing the concerns and problems of marginalized groups, as well as offer them legitimate opportunities to learn how to negotiate, influence, and work within the larger system. According to Cohen, these secondary associations

> do not naturally arise, either for the purposes of addressing problems of underrepresentation or for more functional tasks: There is, for example, no natural tendency for an emergence of secondary associations to correct for inequalites of political opportunity due to underlying economic inequalities or to ensure the regulatory competence needed to advance the common good.[13]

Therefore, a "strategy of associative democracy" is necessary to foster the types of secondary associations that would be capable of "(a) representing previously underrepresented interests, and (b) advancing regulatory competence."[14]

Smith argues that deliberative democracy provides a model for those charter schools that claim democratic participation as a central focus of their missions. The model can be used by charter groups and sponsors to assess how well an organization balances "a plurality of interests in public education," employs governance procedures that "result in legitimate collective decisions," and promotes "regulatory competence" in citizens (136). For parent-run charters, this theory could be helpful in all stages of the organization's development; from the creation of governance and organizational systems during the pre-petition phase through the operational life of the organization.

NOTES

1. RPP, *Charter Schools,* 1999.

2. Casey, 1995; cited by Eugene Bardach, *Getting Agencies to Work Together: The Practice and Theory of Managerial Craftsmanship* (Washington, DC: Brookings Institution, 1998).

3. J. D. Thompson and A. Tuden, "Strategies, Structures and Processes of Organizational Decision," in *Comparative Studies in Administration,* ed. J. D. Thompson (Pittsburgh: University of Pittsburgh Press, 1956), 195–216, cited by Butler in "Time in Organizations."

4. Karl E. Weick, *The Social Psychology of Organizing,* 2d ed. (Reading, MA: Addison-Wesley Publishing Company, 1979).

5. Ibid., 198.

6. Bardach, *Getting Agencies to Work Together,* 282.

7. Butler, "Time in Organizations," 935.

8. B. Rollier and J. A. Turner, "Planning Forward by Looking Backward: Retrospective Thinking in Strategic Decision-making," *Decision Sciences* 25.2 (1994): 169–88, cited by Butler in "Time in Organizations."

9. Sergiovanni, 1994, p. xiii.

10. Stacy Smith, "Charter Schools: Voluntary Associations or Political Communities?" in *Philosophy of Education,* ed. S. Tozer (Urbana: University of Illinois at Urbana-Champaign, 1998), 131–39; Stacy Smith, *The Democratic Potential of Charter Schools* (New York: Peter Lang Publishing, in press).

11. Smith, "Charter Schools," 136. Smith cites Joshua Cohen, "Procedure and Substance in Deliberative Democracy," in *Democracy and Difference: Contesting the Boundaries of the*

Political, ed. Seyla Benhabib (Princeton, NJ: Princeton University Press, 1996), 95–119, 112.

12. Seyla Benhabib, *Situating the Self: Gender, Community, and Postmodernism in Contemporary Ethics* (New York: Routledge, 1992), 111.

13. Cohen, "Procedure and Substance," 110.

14. Smith, "Charter Schools," 135.

CONCLUSION

Staffing, enrollment, and finances stabilized at C-Star by the fourth year of operations, but the charter school continues to wrestle with the issues of parent involvement and internal democracy. Two of the original founding group of parents remain employed at the school; James as head teacher, Evelyn as office administrator.

Community Charter never recovered from its initial years of struggle. By the Fall of 1999, all of the founding families had exited the school, enrollment numbers were down substantially, and staff turnover was a chronic condition. The Community Charter parent board of directors and the administration clashed repeatedly over who had the final say on operating and curriculum decisions. In the early Spring of 2000, Warren County revoked the school's charter citing the operation's "questionable long-term viability" as the primary reason for the decision.

Considering the complexity of a charter operation, it appears that parent participation and governance will remain at the forefront of a parent-run charter school's concerns, even with a parent contract in place and a strategy for implementation.

The following are themes that emerged from this study.

- Building a charter school community governed collectively by parents should not be idealized or used as a marketing tool to attract families. Underestimating the importance of clearly defining "parent-run" or "parent co-op" appears to be a setup for future internal conflict.

- In the beginning, the founding process can be *organic* and conducive to community building and collective organizing. There is more time available for brainstorming, socializing, and forging consensus among group members. Once the petition process begins—and lobbying, politicking, and meeting external demands move to the forefront—the organizational experience becomes more *strategic* and requires a different type of expertise and skills from the membership to move the organization forward. After approval, the nature of the work evolves again, with many complex and critical tasks having to be addressed simultaneously in order to open the school. Decision making after approval can become opportunistic or rash in order to move toward this goal. A democratic process can seem interminably slow during this period and the desire to move things along can promote group acceptance of one or two members taking hold of the situation and securing very powerful roles for themselves in the organizational structure.

- The overseeing of complex tasks in the post-approval through operations phases of a charter school's development appears to demand that one person or a team of individuals be invested with "the authority—the legitimate right—to make demands, exert influence, and impose sanctions."[1] However, systems and processes must be in place for the group to hold its leaders accountable.

- Those individuals who take on leadership roles in parent-run charter schools acquire a level of knowledge about the organization that impacts their relationships with staff and other parents. From their vantage point as leaders, facets of the organization are more visible to them (e.g., the relationships of enrollment to financial stability, and accountability to the educational program) than to other parents and staff. This can cause boards and administrators of charters to adopt the frame of mind of *service organization* decision-makers ruling for clients who are ignorant of the big picture.

- Because of the history and knowledge that founders possess of their charter school, it may be hard for them to transition out of roles of power in the organization. Although the struggle for power may not be a conscious or deliberate act, power can become a central feature that can be "self-defeating for all participants."[2]

- The degree of difficulty that external barriers impose on start-ups is impacted by founders' educational and economic backgrounds, work experiences, and social and professional networks.

- The interplay of external factors and a charter's founding vision appears to be ongoing throughout the life of a charter school—at least through the first years of operations. "Circumstances change."[3] Political context, neighborhood demographics, personnel, and student population are just some of the factors that can change over time. Regulations or specifics that sponsors may impose might also have implications on the founding vision that need to be addressed before operations begin.

- The location and physical plant of a charter school facility can have many implications. Is the facility far from the population the charter will be serving? Is there easy access to public transportation? Are there plans for expansion that would render the facility unusable within three to five years? Not seriously considering questions such as these can result in operators wrestling with student turnover, recruitment, major restructuring of the educational program, or relocation during the critical first years of operation.

- Minimal start-up funding is a serious barrier to organizational health. Two critical ways in which it can impact the school are:

    - Not being able to hire staff long before operations begin. This makes it difficult for planning and for teachers and administrators to establish collegial working relationships with each other. It also can result in last-minute, desperate attempts to find teachers and support staff who may not be qualified applicants.

    - Minimal technology and the means to accomplish the work that needs to be done. This not only impacts efficiency, but also determines who can contribute effectively to the founding process. Parents who have personal access to technology and resources, and those who have the time to volunteer, can assume powerful roles in a grassroots charter school.

- The reasons why parents enroll their children in a parent-run charter school may not have anything to do with the founding vision of the school. Parents may be choosing the school simply because of the location or their lack of other choices.

- Parents not participating in charter school meetings and activities does not necessarily mean that the membership is apathetic. It could be an indication that parents do not know how to participate in the process or that their home situations are preventing involvement. It could also mean that strategies or avenues for involvement are limited.

According to decision-making theorists, a certain amount of "groping along and trial-and-error learning"[4] or "muddling through"[5] is inevitable in a new enterprise that is bucking the status quo. In addition, as Karl Weick argues, trial and error can supply the data necessary for a reflective organizational process.[6] Considering the experiences of the parent groups in this study, the following are some suggestions that may be helpful for future charter organizers.

- Establishing a partnership with an established, local community nonprofit, university, or community college prior to petitioning the sponsor. This could enable charter founders to secure loans for start-up and provide some local political support for their venture.

- Instituting parent involvement requirements as a condition of enrollment; or taking strategic steps to convince a reluctant sponsor about the implications of not having requirements in a charter school where parent involvement is central to the vision. Parent requirements can provide a foundation on which to build community. Without an enforceable contract, it appears that chances are just too great for unequal participation to create factions among parents. This situation can lead to internal conflicts that can threaten a charter school's stability and ability to meet its obligation of educating students. It is important to be aware, however, that parent contracts will not automatically solve the problems of maintaining internal democracy, which will have to be addressed as an ongoing mission of the organization.

The other critical issue that must be addressed by charter founders and sponsors in considering the adoption of parent contracts is the possibility of this tool being used as a method of exclusion. Current research has not uncovered concrete evidence of exclusion through the use of contracts; nevertheless, charter sponsors, founders, and operators should be aware of the potential for abuse and probe the motivation behind adopting the policy. Periodic evaluations of the implementation strategies employed should also be instituted.

- Employing decision-making strategies such as Karl Weick's *retrospective sense-making* or "thinking in the future perfect tense."[7] Decision-making aids that help founders to consider future implications of their decisions and policies can assist in separating the core elements of the charter vision from strategies for implementation.

- Creating and instituting a means for the parents to learn how to participate, make decisions, and govern. For charter schools that are attempting to adopt or adapt a *mutual-benefit* type of structure where parents chart policy and make decisions collectively for the organization, this is crucial so that power can be passed along to newer members and shared among a broader cross-section of the parent membership.

- Strategizing early on in the developmental process about staff. Finding and adequately compensating an effective staff who are committed to the vision of a parent-run charter is paramount. Perhaps approaching teacher education colleges and universities to establish internships and placements for teacher researchers and student teachers could be a long-term strategy for charter schools. It seems logical to start building a foundation for the development of teachers and administrators in the particularities of decentralized, alternative public schools.

For Weick, shaping attitudes and developing individuals' abilities to reflectively view actions and make sense of them may be more important to increased efficiency and long-term stability than a founder's complex organizational plan.[8] But key questions remain: How do you shape attitudes and change the behaviors among the adults in a charter school in a way that will further participation and involvement? How do you balance this work with educating students? These are critical questions for founders of *mutual-benefit* grassroots charter schools to discuss—among themselves and supporters, as well as with critics and sponsors. It is folly not to actively address this potential dilemma with some strategic planning.

I agree with Smith in that "charters provide the possibility of a proliferation of quite distinct schools within the public educational sphere."[9] Parent-run charter schools—taking into account their own mix of local and state, social and political factors—have the unique opportunity to influence for themselves the formal practice of schooling, as well as play a role in reshaping the larger concept of public education. There are restrictions and barriers still, but the fact is: The circle of those eligible to start public schools has been widened. This is a challenge to traditional power relationships within the public education system, and between the system and the community.

As Sarason cautions, however, challenging traditional power relationships is one thing; implementing the change is quite another matter.[10] Conflict appears inevitable. However, this does not mean that change should be abandoned or that one is without means to lessen conflict's unproductive consequences. Thinking outside the box that has bounded educational practice for a century is an enormous task. "What is at stake is not power in and of itself but the concrete ways by which alterations of power will in turn alter the ecology of classrooms, schools, and their surrounding communities."[11]

NOTES

1. Newton and Levinson, "The Work Group," 126.
2. Sarason, *Parental Involvement*, 28.
3. Bardach, *Getting Agencies to Work Together*.
4. Ibid.
5. C. Lindbloom, "The Science of Muddling Through," *Public Administration Review* 19 (1959): 79–88, cited in Butler, "Time in Organizations," 935.
6. Weick, *The Social Psychology of Organizing*, 2nd ed.
7. Ibid.
8. Ibid.
9. Smith, "Charter Schools," 131.
10. Sarason, *Parental Involvement*.
11. Ibid., 12.

APPENDIXES

Appendix A. Data Collection Specifics: C-Star

Year One Observations and Interviews

1. Participant observation (60 hours)

I assisted teachers with children in the art studio, kindergarten, and first-grade classrooms one full day per week for seven months. Parents were observed volunteering in the classrooms, before and after school dropping off and picking up their children, and interacting with staff. Field notes were recorded during natural pauses and breaks throughout the day.

2. Nonparticipant observation (42 hours)

Seven after-school staff meetings (20 hours); six evening parent meetings (15 hours); and two board meetings (7 hours) were attended in the first seven months. The majority of parent meetings, board meetings, and staff meetings were audiotaped. Field notes were also taken. Only two parent meetings and one staff meeting were not audiotaped; field notes were recorded.

3. Interviews (44)

STAFF (N = 6). The core staff included three paid (kindergarten teacher, first-grade teacher/educational leader, and art teacher) and two unpaid staff members (student teacher and administrative assistant/chief parent volunteer). The administrative assistant began her duties as a parent volunteer but was eventually hired as a full-time employee. In the last three months of school, a parent who was a substitute teacher in the district replaced the first-grade teacher.

Unstructured and semistructured interviews with open-ended questions to allow for personal stories and reflection were initially conducted with three staff members (art teacher, student teacher, and administrative assistant). These interviews took place on-site or by phone with note-taking being the primary method of record keeping.

After this series of exploratory interviews, more formal, structured interviews with questions concentrating specifically on experiences concerning the planning stage and the first three months of operations were then scheduled with four staff members (art teacher, first-grade teacher/educational leader, student teacher, and administrative assistant). Three of the interviews were audiotaped and took place off-site. Notes were taken during a series of phone interviews with the administrative assistant. Four follow-up interviews, two on-site and two by phone, were conducted.

The kindergarten teacher was not formally interviewed due to schedule conflicts and illness. However, more time was spent as a participant-observer in this teacher's classroom (compared to the other classrooms), and an off-site, informal 45-minute conversation was held with her. The teacher requested that the conversation not be audiotaped, so only field notes were taken.

The substitute first-grade teacher was not interviewed until the following school year.

PARENTS AND GUARDIANS (N = 43 families). Unstructured interviews with open-ended questions to allow for personal stories and reflection were initially conducted with four parent volunteers (the total number of parent volunteers fluctuated substantially over the course of the research). These parent volunteers were targeted because of their high degree of participation. Interviews took place on-site during school hours; field notes were taken.

Informal interviews were also conducted randomly with 15 parents on-site during school hours and at parent meetings throughout the first school year. Notes were taken during these on-the-spot interviews or immediately following the conversations.

Five parents were selected for formal interviewing; three were audiotaped and in two cases, field notes were taken. These informants were chosen as a result of the initial informal interviews and/or after observing their actions and comments at parent meetings. The selection of parent informants was also influenced by observations of their interactions with the staff during school hours and by comments made by staff members about parents.

Ten parents who chose to disenroll their children were interviewed over the phone during the summer months. Handwritten notes were taken.

DISTRICT PERSONNEL AND SCHOOL BOARD MEMBERS. Two interviews, one by phone and one in person, were conducted with two school board members. Three interviews were conducted with district staff. Notes were handwritten.

Year Two Observations and Interviews

1. Nonparticipant observation (44 hours)

Eight meetings—a combination of board, parent, and weekend work meetings focusing on strategic planning and teacher evaluations—were attended for a total of 28 hours. Two school days were spent on-site observing parents dropping off/picking up their children, with students and teachers in the classrooms, in the office, or on the school yard (16 hours).

Board meetings and weekend work meetings were audiotaped. Field notes were also taken. Parent meetings were held in the art studio and due to the poor acoustics, they were not audiotaped; field notes were handwritten.

2. Interviews (24)

STAFF (N = 4). The core staff included three paid teachers (K, 1/2, and art teacher) and one office administrator. Two teachers were new as of this year. The office administrator was interviewed by phone; notes were recorded. Teachers were observed during meetings, in the classroom, or on the school yard, and conversations were held on site. One teacher was interviewed by phone.

FORMER STAFF MEMBERS. Two former staff members were interviewed over the phone. Notes were handwritten.

An educational consultant who was hired to assist in evaluating staff was interviewed over the phone. Notes were handwritten.

PARENTS (N = 40 families). Six parents were informally interviewed at the school, before or after meetings. Five parents were interviewed by phone. Four parents from Year One, who had chosen not to enroll their children in Year Two, were interviewed by phone. Two off-site interviews with the board president were conducted. Field notes were taken for all interviews, except for the board president's, which was audiotaped.

DISTRICT PERSONNEL AND SCHOOL BOARD MEMBERS. One phone interview was conducted with a school board member and two with district staff. Notes were handwritten.

Documents Reviewed

The documents reviewed that were particular to this case study included:

- The operating charter, bylaws, meeting minutes, and weekly "parent folders" containing current school news and correspondence.

- Local newspaper articles about C-Star.
- The operating charters of five other California schools: a public conversion school and a start-up within the research site's district, and three start-up schools in neighboring districts.
- Local school district documents on the charter school approval process.

Appendix B. Data Collection Specifics: Community Charter

Year One Observations and Interviews

1. Participant and nonparticipant observation (72.5 hours)

I attended seven general meetings (18 hours), eight interim board meetings (20 hours), one by-law committee meeting (2.5 hours), three work/process meetings (4 hours), two orientations (4 hours each), and six curriculum committee meetings (10 hours). Meetings were audiotaped when sound conditions were optimal; handwritten notes were also taken. In meetings where audiotaping was not possible, only field notes were recorded. Meeting minutes that were recorded by a charter school member were also collected.

Two informal, information-gathering meetings with charter members (2 hours) were also attended by the researcher. Field notes were taken at these meetings.

Two county board of education meetings were attended: One session was for the general purpose of observing county board members and the superintendent; the purpose of the second session was the public hearing for Community Charter's petition. Field notes were recorded. The county hearing was also videotaped by a charter school parent.

2. Interviews (32)

PARENTS AND COMMUNITY MEMBERS. The number of parents and community members in the charter school working group fluctuated greatly in the first two years of data collection.

I conversed with members frequently by phone and in person during the first year. The first face-to-face interviews were semistructured, with open-ended questions to allow for personal stories and reflection. Questions posed to Community Charter members during these interviews concentrated on their motivation for organizing or joining the group, how they viewed their role within the group, negotiations with the district and the prior petition hearings, and/or the overall experience of being involved in a grassroots, start-up charter school. Interviews were audiotaped and transcribed. In addition to "spontaneous" phone calls and casual conversations, thirteen formal interviews were conducted by phone or in person and thirteen informal interviews took place before or after meetings.

DISTRICT, COUNTY, AND UNION PERSONNEL. Phone interviews were conducted with two staff members of the local school district, one staff member from the county board of education, one staff member of the local teachers union, and two local public school teachers/union members. These interviews were formal and structured, with questions focusing on charter schools in general, the role of the sponsor, and Community Charter's petition. Handwritten notes were taken.

Year Two Observations and Interviews

1. Nonparticipant observation (25 hours)

Three meetings were attended and four site visits were made. One visit was for the purpose of viewing the interim school setup; the second was a walking tour of the immediate neighborhood; the third, to observe a community outreach day held at the school; the fourth, to observe a clean-up/work/renovation day. Notes were handwritten.

2. Interviews (20)

PARENTS. Phone interviews were held with 15 members who had left the group and 3 parents who were either involved in the interim school or charter work. Notes were handwritten.

COUNTY PERSONNEL. Phone interviews were conducted with two staff members of the county. Interviews were audiotaped.

Year Three Observations and Interviews

1. Nonparticipant observation (15 hours)

Four site visits were made to the school. One visit was the day before school opened, to observe and interview staff; the second was back-to-school night; the third and fourth were to observe staff and parents in the classrooms. One site visit was made to a fund-raising event off-site. Field notes were handwritten.

2. Interviews (23)

PARENTS (N = 60 families). Six parents were interviewed at the school site; three were interviewed off-site. Seven parents were interviewed by phone. Two interviews were audiotaped; for others, notes were handwritten.

STAFF (N = 6). Five staff members (teachers and coordinators) were interviewed on-site. Notes were handwritten.

COUNTY PERSONNEL. A phone interview was conducted with one staff member at the county office and one face-to-face interview took place with one board member. Handwritten notes were taken.

Documents Reviewed

Drafts and final versions of school documents (charter, bylaws, position statements, manuals of operation, etc.) were collected and reviewed. Documents that were particular to this case study included:

- Operating charter, meeting minutes, manuals of operation, correspondence between the sponsor and the charter group, advertisements, grant applications, informational mailings to potential parents, communication between school and parents.
- Local newspaper articles about Community Charter.
- The operating charters of seven other California schools: a public conversion school and a start-up within the research site's district, and five start-up schools in neighboring districts.

Documents were a major source of data in Years Two and Three.

GLOSSARY

Charter opportunity space. State charter laws vary considerably, reflecting the politics and the history of educational reform in a state, as well as the relationships between the state and its school districts. These factors profoundly affect the number and types of charter schools allowed in the state, how they operate, and their potential impact on the surrounding schools. Paul Berman explains that "a state's charter legislation and the regulations that grow up around that legislation have a profound effect on the charter development and charter granting process. The de jure situation mandated by law may differ from the de facto reality of how the laws are administered and implemented."[1] State and local social-political factors create an "opportunity space" for charter developers; hence the vast differences in types of charter schools from state to state, district to district, and even neighborhood to neighborhood.

Cui bono. Blau and Scott's classificatory scheme of organizations based on the question of "who benefits?" in the organization. The four types of organizations that result from the application of this criterion are:

- *Mutual-benefit associations,* where the prime beneficiary is the membership;

- *Business concerns*, where the owners are the prime beneficiary;
- *Service organizations*, where the client group is the prime beneficiary; and
- *Commonweal organizations*, where the prime beneficiary is the public at large.[2]

Cultural capital. Pierre Bourdieu defines the concept of cultural capital as the overall cultural background, makeup, ways of living, knowledge, and skills that are passed on from generation to generation. In his theory, children of the upper classes inherit a very different cultural capital than working-class children.[3] Children who grow up in families that frequent museums, read books, have libraries in the home, attend live theater, and enjoy other cultural activities acquire a familiarity with the dominant culture that is valued by schools. Children whose families are on the margins and do not engage in such practices, or engage in them infrequently, are at a disadvantage.

Culture. Core values, assumptions, and beliefs that provide a framework for group development and action. The *social structure* of an organization or working group "tends to reflect underlying cultural values and helps to realize those values. *Culture* and *social structure* tend to be relatively congruent." However, in an organization such as a start-up charter school, the degree of congruence can be tenuous. "Over time, changes in the one are likely to produce changes in the other."[4]

Ethos and values. Vision; deep beliefs. The following are some of the questions that frame the *National Study of Charter Schools'* investigation of *ethos and values* in field sample charter schools. The questions reveal the foundational role that *ethos and values* can play in the mission and educational program of a charter school.

- What are the distinguishing characteristics of the guiding beliefs and how coherent and shared are they?
- How does the school staff describe the school's vision? How do parents? Students?

- How important is the vision/mission in the everyday life of the school?
- How coherently is the vision being implemented?
- Have important elements of the vision/mission of the school become modified over time? If so, how and why?[5]

Likemindedness. Dewey believed that the nucleus of a community is formed by shared "aims, beliefs, aspirations, knowledge—a common understanding. ...Such things cannot be passed physically from one to another, like bricks; they cannot be shared as persons would share a pie by dividing it into physical pieces. The communication which insures participation in a common understanding is one which secures similar emotional and intellectual dispositions—like ways of responding to expectations and requirements."[6]

Organic solidarity. Mutual trust and common understanding. See *organic time.*[7]

Organic time. A "collective type" of organizational model that both C-Star and Community Charter parents envisioned relies heavily on the development of trust.[8] The time line or time frame for developing this type of organization should be nonlinear and *organic,* to allow for ideas to generate and decisions to be forged through consensus. According to Butler, an important aspect of time in a collective model is the extent to which it allows this atmosphere of mutual trust and common understanding to grow. In coining this term Butler alludes to the natural growth of plants to highlight "the need to tend to the general environment of the process, such as the need to tend to the general environment of processes, through feeding and nourishing, rather than through direction and control"(933).

Retrospective sense-making. "Thinking in the future perfect tense," a decision-making strategy that Karl Weick proposes for organizational managers when speculating about the future effects of a present decision. According to Weick, "If one is able to treat a future event as if it's already over and done, then presumably it's easier to write a specific history based on past experience that could generate that specific outcome. The future event is more sensible because you can visualize at least one prior set of means that will produce it. The meaning of that end *is* [his emphasis] those means that bring it about.[9]

Role-conception. A definition and rationale for one's position within the structure that is formed partially within the given organization. An individual's ideas about his or her role are influenced by "childhood experiences, by his (her) values and other personality characteristics, by formal education and apprenticeship and the like."[10]

Role-definition. Operating within a "complex system of requirements, facilities, and conditions of work, the individual effects his modes of adaptation."[11] There are two levels of adaptation: the ideational (*role-conception*) and the behavioral (*role-performance*).

Role-demands are situational pressures that confront the individual as the occupant of a given structural position. The sources of these pressures are "in the official charter and policies of the organization; in the traditions and ideology, explicit as well as implicit, that help to define the organization's purposes and modes of operation; in the views about this position which are held by members of the position (who influence any single member) and by members of the various positions impinging upon this one."[12]

Role-dilemmas. Contradictions experienced by individuals in their given positions, such as conflicting pressure between home life demands and school involvement.[13]

Role-facilities. The means made available to individuals to fulfill organizational duties, such as technology, resources, and conditions of work.[14]

Role-performance is the result of a number of forces. Some of these forces are external, such as the *role-demands* of a particular position and pressure from one's superiors in an organization. Informal group influences and impending sanctions can impact *role-performance*. Other determinants are internal, such as one's *role-conceptions* and personality traits that are relevant to the particular role.[15]

Role-requirements are usually defined as assigned tasks, rules governing relationships and output, and so on. However, in "attempting to characterize the role requirements for a given position, one must ... guard against the assumption that they are unified and logically coherent. There may be major differences and even contradictions between official norms, as defined by charter or by administrative authority, and the 'information' norms held by various groupings within the organization."[16]

Social process. "How a group works ... from the highly rational forms of planning, problem solving, and collaborative use of technical skills to the most irrational forms of destruction of any real work as well as exploitation and humiliation of members."[17] Recurring themes are important. Widely shared feelings and fantasies about collective life, as well as what the group actually does, create the *social process*. "Often, group members are so submerged in the process that dominant themes go unnoticed."[18]

Social structure. In utilizing this term, Newton & Levinson emphasize two components of structure: the division of labor and the division of authority. In more formal organizations, positions are formally defined and permanent; they are typically changed through a redefinition of organizational structure, not through the comings and goings of individuals. Individuals in formally structured working groups occupy positions and take roles. *Role-performance* is structurally based in requirements that accompany a given position. However, even in formal working groups, requirements are usually ambiguous enough to allow the individual *role-performance* to be shaped also by the personality and background experience of the individual worker. The more roles and tasks there are, the more need there is for activities to be integrated and coordinated. In order to do this, someone must have the responsibility for this ordering and coordination. "Responsibility requires that one have the authority—the legitimate right—to make demands, exert influence, and impose sanctions. Organizations are stratified in order to achieve the integration necessary to the fulfillment of complex tasks."[19]

Spasmodic time. "The present is experienced through events that are irregular, highly novel, movable, and with many concurrent events also impinging." There may be disagreement as to what the goals of the organization are; a lack of codified rules on how to move forward; and/or minimal staff capacity or technology to meet external demands.[20]

Strategic time. Organizational time as experienced in "games, markets, and politics" where one player's action is followed by a reaction on the part of the opposition. The first player has to await the move by the opposition in order to know what to do next. One must be able to think strategically in order to participate effectively. "The past provides codes as to how moves can be made and provides participants with bases of power from which to act."[21]

NOTES

1. Paul Berman, "Charter schools: A Partial and Imperfect Market System of Public Education," paper prepared for "Education between State and Civil Society," Emeryville, CA, 1997, 3.
2. Blau and Scott, *Formal Organizations*, 43.
3. Bourdieu, "Cultural Reproduction."
4. Newton and Levinson, "The Work Group," 130–31.
5. National Study of Charter Schools, *Field Brief Guide*, 1997.
6. Dewey, *Democracy and Education 1916*, 7.
7. Butler, "Time in Organizations."
8. Ibid.
9. Weick, *Social Psychology*, 1979 ed., 198.
10. Levinson, "Roles, Personality, and Social Structure," 176.
11. Ibid., 175.
12. Ibid., 173.
13. Ibid., 170–80.
14. Ibid.
15. Ibid.
16. Ibid., 174.
17. Newton and Levinson, "The Work Group," 117.

18. Ibid., 134.

19. Ibid., 126.

20. Butler, "Time in Organizations."

21. Ibid., 933–34.

BIBLIOGRAPHY

Anyon, Jean. "Race, Social Class, and Educational Reform in an Inner City School." *Teachers College Record* 97.1 (1990): 69–94.

Bardach, Eugene. *Getting Agencies to Work Together: The Practice and Theory of Managerial Craftsmanship.* Washington, DC: Brookings Institution, 1998.

Baron, J. and J. C. Hershey. "Outcome Bias in Decision Evaluation." *Journal of Personality and Social Psychology* 34 (1988): 240–47.

Battistich, Victor, Daniel Solomon, Dong-il Kim, Marilyn Watson, and Eric Schaps. "Schools as Communities, Poverty Levels of Student Populations, and Students' Attitudes, Motives, and Performance: A Multilevel Analysis." *American Educational Research Journal* 32.3 (1995): 627–58.

Becker, Henry J., Kathryn Nakagawa, and Ronald G. Corwin. *Parent Involvement Contracts in California's Charter Schools: Strategy for Educational Improvement or Method of Exclusion?* Los Alamitos, CA: Southwest Regional Laboratory, 1995.

Benhabib, Seyla. *Situating the Self: Gender, Community and Postmodernism in Contemporary Ethics.* New York: Routledge, 1992.

Berman, Paul. "Charter Schools: A Partial and Imperfect Market System of Public Education." Paper prepared for Education between State and Civil Society, Emeryville, CA, 1997.

Blau, Peter M., and W. Richard Scott. *Formal Organizations: A Comparative Approach.* San Francisco: Chandler Publishing Company, 1962.

Bourdieu, Pierre. "Cultural Reproduction and Social Reproduction." In *Power and Ideology in Education*, edited by J. Karabel and A. H. Halsey. New York: Oxford University Press, 1977.

Bradley, A. "Allies for Education." *Education Week* (Sept. 4, 1996): 43–46.

Bronfenbrenner, Urie. *Is Early Intervention Effective: A Report on Longitudinal Evaluations of Preschool Programs.* Vol. 2. Washington, DC: Department of Health, Education, and Welfare, 1974.

Brouillette, Liane. *A Geology of School Reform: The Successive Restructurings of a School District.* Albany: State University of New York, 1996.

Butler, Richard. "Time in Organizations: Its Experience, Explanations and Effects." *Organization Studies* 16.6 (1995): 925–50.

Cohen, Joshua. "Deliberation and Democratic Legitimacy." In *The Good Polity: Normative Analysis of the State*, edited by Alan Hamlin and Philip Pettit, 17–34. London: Blackwell, 1989.

—. "Procedure and Substance in Deliberative Democracy." In *Democracy and Difference: Contesting the Boundaries of the Political,* edited by Seyla Benhabib, 95–119. Princeton: Princeton University Press, 1996.

Cohen, M. D., J. G. March, and P. J. Olsen. "A Garbage-Can Model of Organizational Choice." *Administrative Science Quarterly* 17.1 (1972): 1–25.

Coleman, James. "Families and Schools." *Educational Researcher* 16 (1987): 32–38.

Coleman, James E., and Thomas Hoffer. *Public and Private High Schools: The Impact of Communities.* New York: Basic Books, 1987.

Comer, James P. *School Power.* New York: New York University Press, 1980.

—. "Educating Poor Minority Children." *Scientific American* 259 (1988): 42–48.

Corwin, Ronald G., Lisa Carlos, Bart Lagomarsino, and Roger Scott. "From Paper to Practice: Challenges Facing a California Charter School." Executive Summary. San Francisco: WestEd, May 1996.

Corwin, Ronald G., and John F. Flaherty, eds. *Freedom and Innovation in California's Charter Schools.* Southwest Regional Laboratory, 1995.

Dauber, Susan L., and Joyce L. Epstein. "Parents' Attitudes and Practices of Involvement in Inner-City Elementary and Middle Schools." In *Families and Schools in a Pluralistic Society,* edited by Nancy F. Chavkin, 53–71. Albany: State University of New York Press, 1993.

Delgado-Gaitan, Concha. "Involving Parents in the Schools: A Process of Empowerment." *American Journal of Education* 100.1 (1991): 20–46.

—. "School Matters in the Mexican-American Home: Socializing Children to Education." *American Educational Research Journal* 29.3 (1992): 495–513.

Dewey, John. *Democracy and Education 1916.* Carbondale: Southern Illinois University Press, 1985.

Dianda, Marcella R., and Ronald G. Corwin. *Vision and Reality: A First-Year Look at California's Charter Schools.* Southwest Regional Laboratory, 1994.

Durkheim, Emil. *Suicide: A Study in Sociology,* translated by J. A. Spalding and G. Simpson. Originally published in 1897. New York: Free Press, 1951.

—. *The Division of Labor in Society,* translated by G. Simpson Originally published in 1893. New York: Free Press, 1964.

Edwards, Carolyn, Leila Gandini, and George Forman. *The Hundred Languages of Children.* Norwood, NJ: Ablex Publishing Corporation, 1993.

Epstein, Joyce L., and Susan L. Dauber. "Teacher Attitudes and Practices of Parent Involvement in Inner-City Elementary and Middle Schools." Paper presented at the annual meeting of the American Sociological Association, Atlanta, GA, 1988.

Erickson, Frederick. "Qualitative Methods in Research on Teaching." In *Handbook of Research on Teaching,* edited by Merlin C. Wittrock. 3rd ed., 119–69. London: Collier MacMillan 1985.

Fine, Michelle. "[Ap]parent Involvement: Reflections on Parents, Power, and Urban Public Schools." *Teachers College Record* 94.4 (1993): 682–710.

Fuller, Bruce. "Which School Reforms are Politically Sustainable and Locally Effective? The Contextual Influence of Cultural Pluralism." Paper presented at the University of California, Berkeley, Graduate School of Education, April 1995.

Fuller, Bruce, and Richard F. Elmore, eds. *Who Chooses? Who Loses? Culture, Institutions, and the Unequal Effects of School Choice.* New York: Teachers College Press, 1996.

Haberman, Martin. "Creating Community Contexts That Educate: An Agenda for Improving Education in Inner Cities." In *Education and the Family,* edited by Leonard Kaplan, 27–40. Needham Heights, NJ: Allyn and Bacon, 1992.

Habermas, Jürgen. "Three Normative Models of Democracy." In *Democracy and Difference: Contesting the Boundaries of the Political,* edited by Seyla Benhabib, 21–30. Princeton: Princeton University Press, 1996.

Hawkins, Scott A., and Reid Hastie. "Hindsight: Judgements of Past Events After the Outcomes Are Known." *Psychological Review* 107 (1990): 311–27.

Henderson, Anne. *The Evidence Continues to Grow: Parent Involvement Improves Student Achievement.* Columbia, MD: National Committee for Citizens in Education, 1987.

Henig, Jeffrey R. "The Local Dynamics of Choice: Ethnic Preferences and Institutional Responses." In *Who Chooses? Who Loses? Culture, Institutions, and the Unequal Effects of School Choice*, edited by Bruce Fuller and Richard F. Elmore, 95–117. New York: Teachers College Press, 1996.

Hilfiker, Leo R. "Factors Relating to the Innovativeness of School Systems." *Journal of Educational Research* 64.1 (1970): 23–27.

Houston, W. R., and E. Houston. "Needed: A New Knowledge Base in Teacher Education." In *Education and the Family,* edited by Leonard Kaplan, 255–65. Needham Heights, NJ: Allyn and Bacon, 1992.

Houston, W. R., and J. L. Williamson. *Perceptions of Their Preparation by 42 Texas Elementary School Teachers Compared with Their Responses as Student Teachers.* Houston, TX: University of Houston, 1990.

Kantor, Harvey. "Equal Opportunity and the Federal Role in Education." *Rethinking Schools,* 11.2 (1996/97, Winter): 8–12.

Kapel, D. E., and W. T. Pink. "The Schoolboard: Participatory Democracy Revisited." *Urban Review* 10 (1978): 20–34.

Kirst, Michael W. "Who's in Charge? Federal, State, and Local Control." In *Learning from the Past,* edited by Diane Ravitch and Maris A. Vinovskis. Baltimore: Johns Hopkins University Press, 1995.

Kochan, F., and B. K. Mullins. "Teacher Education: Linking Universities, Schools, and Families for the 21st Century." In *Education and the Family,* edited by Leonard Kaplan, 266–72. Needham Heights, NJ: Allyn and Bacon, 1992.

Kohn, M. S. "Social Class and Parent-Child Relationships." In *Sociology of the Family,* edited by M. Anderson. Middlesex, UK: Penguin Books, 1971.

Koppich, Julia E. "Choice in Education: Not Whether, But What?" *Educator* 8.1 (1994): 2–7.

——. "How Californians View Public Education." *Educator* 8.1 (1994): 18–23.

Lareau, Annette. *Home Advantage: Social Class and Parental Intervention in Elementary Education.* New York: Falmer, 1989.

Latane, B., K. Williams, and S. Harkins, "Many Hands Make Light Work: The Causes and Consequences of Social Loafing." *Journal of Personality and Social Psychology* 37 (1977): 822–32.

LeBlanc, P. "Parent-School Interactions. In *Education and the Family,* edited by Leonard Kaplan, 132–40. Needham Heights, NJ: Allyn and Bacon, 1992.

Levinson, Daniel J. "Roles, Personality, and Social Structure in the Organizational Setting." *Journal of Abnormal and Normal Social Psychology* 59 (1959): 170–80.

Lindbloom, C. "The Science of Muddling Through." *Public Administration Review* 19 (1959): 79–88.

MacMillan, David W., and David M. Chavis. "Sense of Community: A Definition and Theory." *Journal of Community Psychology* 14 (1986): 6–23.

Maddaus, J. "Worlds Apart or Links Between: Theoretical Perspectives on Parent-Teacher Relationships." Paper presented at the annual meeting of the American Educational Research Association, Chicago, IL, 1991.

Martinez, Valerie, Kenneth Godwin, and Frank R. Kemerer. "Public School Choice in San Antonio: Who Chooses and with

What Effects?" In *Who Chooses? Who Loses? Culture, Institutions, and the Unequal Effects of School Choice*, edited by Bruce Fuller and Richard F. Elmore, 50–69. New York: Teachers College Press, 1996.

Miles, Matthew B., and A. Michael Huberman. *Qualitative Data Analysis*, 2nd ed. Thousand Oaks, CA: Sage Publications, 1994.

Moles, Oliver C. "Collaboration Between Schools and Disadvantaged Parents: Obstacles and Openings." In *Families and Schools in a Pluralistic Society*, edited by Nancy F. Chavkin, 21–49. Albany: State University of New York Press, 1993.

Nathan, Joe. *Charter Schools: Creating Hope and Opportunity for American Education*. San Francisco: Jossey-Bass Publishers, 1996.

Neuman, Susan B., Tracy Hagedorn, Donna Celano, and Pauline Daly. "Toward a Collaborative Approach to Parent Involvement in Early Education: A Study of Teenage Mothers in an African-American Community." *American Educational Research Journal* 32.4 (1995): 801–27.

Newton, Peter M., and Daniel J. Levinson. "The Work Group within the Organization: A Sociopsychological Approach." *Psychiatry* 36 (1973): 115–42.

Nicholls, A. *Managing Educational Innovations*. London: George Allen & Unwin, 1983.

Office of Civil Rights. *1980 Elementary and Secondary School Survey*. Washington, DC: Office of Civil Rights, US Department of Education, 1982.

Ogbu, John. "Origins of Human Competence: A Cultural-Ecological Perspective." *Child Development* 52 (1981): 413–29.

—. "Understanding Cultural Diversity and Learning." *Educational Researcher* 21.8 (1992): 5–14.

—. "Racial Stratification and Education in the United States: Why Inequality Persists." *Teachers College Record* 96.2 (1994): 264–98.

Olszewski, L., and T. Schevitz. "Classes Packed for Coming Year." *San Francisco Chronicle*. 8 September 1998, 1, 11.

Perry, W., and M. D. Tannenbaum. "Parents, Power, and the Public Schools." In *Education and the Family*, edited by Leonard Kaplan, 100–15. Needham Heights, NJ: Allyn and Bacon, 1992.

Peterson, Paul E. "The New Politics of Choice." In *Learning from the Past: What History Teaches Us about School Reform*, edited by

Diane Ravitch and Maris A. Vinowskis, 217–42. Baltimore: The Johns Hopkins University Press, 1995.

Popkewitz, Thomas S. *A Political Sociology of Educational Reform: Power/Knowledge in Teaching, Teacher Education, and Research.* New York: Teachers College Press, 1991.

Premack, Eric. *California Charter School Revenues, 1994–95: Laying the Foundation for Effectively Managed Independent Public Schools.* California State University, Sacramento: Center for Education Reform, 1994.

——. *1999 Preliminary Overview: New Charter School Funding System, Special Education, and Attendance Accounting Laws*. Sacramento: Charter School Development Center, 1999.

Rasinski, T. V., and A. D. Fredericks. "Working with Parents: Dimensions of Parent Involvement." *The Reading Teacher* 43 (1989): 180–82.

Rofes, Eric. *How Are School Districts Responding to Charter Laws and the Advent of Charter Schools?* Berkeley, CA: Policy Analysis for California Education, 1998.

Rollier, B., and J. A. Turner. "Planning Forward by Looking Backward: Retrospective Thinking in Strategic Decision-making." *Decision Sciences* 25.2 (1994): 169–88.

Rothschild-White, Joyce A. "Conditions Facilitating Participatory-Democratic Organizations." *Sociological Inquiry* 46 (1976): 70–86.

RPP International and the University of Minnesota. *A Study of Charter Schools: Second-Year Report.* Washington, DC: US Department of Education, Office of Educational Research and Improvement, 1998.

RPP International. *A Study of Charter Schools: Third-Year Report.* Washington, DC: US Department of Education, Office of Educational Research and Improvement, 1999.

Salisbury, Robert Holt. *Citizen Participation in the Public Schools.* Lexington, MA: Lexington Books, 1980.

Sarason, Seymour B. *Parental Involvement and the Political Principle: Why the Existing Governance Structure of Public Schools Should Be Abolished.* San Francisco: Jossey-Bass, 1995.

——. *Revisiting "The Culture of the School and the Problem of Change."* New York: Teachers College Press, 1996.

Sergiovanni, Thomas J. *Building Community in Schools.* San Francisco: Jossey-Bass Publishers, 1994.

Shepard, Richard, and Harold Rose. "The Power of Parents: An Empowerment Model for Increasing Parental Involvement." *Education* 115 (1995): 373–77.

Simich-Dudgeon, Carmen. "Increasing Student Achievement Through Teacher Knowledge about Parent Involvement." In *Families and Schools in a Pluralistic Society,* edited by Nancy F. Chavkin, 189–203. Albany: State University of New York Press, 1993.

Smith, Stacy. "Charter Schools: Voluntary Associations or Political Communities?" In *Philosophy of Education,* edited by S. Tozer, 131–39. Urbana: University of Illinois at Urbana-Champaign, 1998.

—. *The Democratic Potential of Charter Schools,* New York: Peter Lang, in press.

Smrekar, Claire. *The Impact of School Choice and Community.* Albany: State University of New York Press, 1996.

Sung, B. L. *Chinese Immigrant Children in New York City.* New York: Center for Migration Studies, 1987.

Swidler, Ann. *Organization without Authority.* Cambridge: Harvard University Press, 1979.

Thompson, J. D., and A. Tuden. "Strategies, Structures and Processes of Organizational Decision." In *Comparative Studies in Administration,* edited by J. D. Thompson, 195–216. Pittsburgh: University of Pittsburgh Press, 1956.

Toomey, D. "Home-School Relations and Inequality in Education." Address to Conference on Education and the Family, Brigham Young University, 1986.

Tran, X. C. *The Factors Hindering Indochinese Parent Participation in School Activities.* San Diego, CA: San Diego State University, Bilingual Education Service Center, Institute for Cultural Pluralism, 1982.

Vanourek, Gregg, Bruno V. Manno, Chester E. Finn, Jr., and Louann A. Bierlein. *Charter Schools in Action. Final Report, Part I.* Washington, D.C.: Hudson Institute, 1997.

Weick, Karl E. *The Social Psychology of Organizing.* 2d ed. Reading, MA: Addison-Wesley Publishing Company, 1979.

Wells, Amy Stuart, Ligia Artiles, Sibyll Carnochan, Camille Wilson Cooper, Cynthia Grutzik, Jennifer Jellison Holme, Alejandra Lopez, Janelle Scott, Julie Slayton, and Ash Vasudeva. *Beyond the Rhetoric of Charter School Reform: A Study of Ten California School Districts*. Los Angeles: UCLA, 1998.

Wissbrun, D., and J. A. Eckart. "Hierarchy of Parental Involvement in Schools." In *Education and the Family*, edited by Leonard Kaplan, 119–31. Needham Heights, NJ: Allyn and Bacon, 1992.

Witte, John F. "Who Benefits from the Milwaukee Choice Program? In *Who Chooses? Who Loses? Culture, Institutions, and the Unequal Effects of School Choice*, edited by Bruce Fuller and Richard F. Elmore, 118–37. New York: Teachers College Press, 1996.

Yancey, Patty. "Parents as Partners in the Organization and Development of Charter Schools." Paper presented at the annual meeting of the American Educational Research Association, Chicago, IL, 1997 (ERIC Document Reproduction Service No. Ps025479).

INDEX

Studies in the Postmodern Theory of Education

General Editors
Joe L. Kincheloe & Shirley R. Steinberg

Counterpoints publishes the most compelling and imaginative books being written in education today. Grounded on the theoretical advances in criticalism, feminism, and postmodernism in the last two decades of the twentieth century, Counterpoints engages the meaning of these innovations in various forms of educational expression. Committed to the proposition that theoretical literature should be accessible to a variety of audiences, the series insists that its authors avoid esoteric and jargonistic languages that transform educational scholarship into an elite discourse for the initiated. Scholarly work matters only to the degree it affects consciousness and practice at multiple sites. Counterpoints' editorial policy is based on these principles and the ability of scholars to break new ground, to open new conversations, to go where educators have never gone before.